THE OFFICIAL BBC SPORT GUIDE
FORMULA ONE 2014

This edition published in 2014
by Carlton Books Limited
20 Mortimer Street
London W1T 3JW

A CIP catalogue record for this book is available from the British Library.

The publisher has taken reasonable steps to check the accuracy of the facts contained herein at the time of going to press, but can take no responsibility for any errors.

ISBN: 978-1-78097-472-9

Senior Editor: Conor Kilgallon
Design Direction: Darren Jordan
Designer: Malcolm Parchment
Production: Maria Petalidou
Picture Research: Paul Langan

Printed in Portugal

Opposite: Lewis Hamilton took his first win for Mercedes at the 2013 Hungarian GP.

THE OFFICIAL BBCSPORT GUIDE

FORMULA ONE 2014

BRUCE JONES

CARLTON

CONTENTS

Right: Red Bull Racing's Sebastian Vettel got to spray champagne a lot in 2013 and will be gunning for a record fifth consecutive title in 2014.

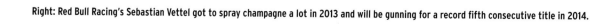

Formula One changes considerably from year to year, but the spectacular setting of Monte Carlo has been the home of the Monaco GP since 1950, a rare constant in a fast-changing sport.

ANALYSIS OF THE 2014 SEASON

It's all change for 2014, with the arrival of new, smaller, turbocharged engines, a revised aerodynamic package, a fuel flow limit and an increase in the amount of energy that can be gathered and reused to boost the cars. With Kimi Raikkonen joining Fernando Alonso at Ferrari and Daniel Ricciardo taking over the seat vacated by Mark Webber at Red Bull Racing, there's also change at two other top teams.

Every fan will be praying that something can be done about Red Bull Racing and Sebastian Vettel as five titles in a row, Schumacher-style, wouldn't be good for Formula One.

With a major rule change dictating that turbocharged engines are back for the first time since 1988, there's definitely the potential for a shake-up of the order of the teams. These V6 turbos offer more torque than the V8s they replace. More important, the energy retrieval systems fitted will offer a greater power boost than before, and for longer each lap.

As became clear in last year's early races, how a team can get its cars to handle on the Pirelli tyres is a huge factor in their performance. Just ask Mercedes and McLaren... For 2014, Pirelli aims to supply new compounds that will improve the racing by ensuring that they don't lead to the performance drop-off that resulted in some drivers cruising around during races, way off their optimum pace, in order to get to the next pitstop.

McLaren's Jenson Button highlighted the predicament when he pointed out, "When we're going around 3s slower than a GP2 car

did in qualifying and only 6s quicker than one in GP3 did in the race, there's something wrong."

More important even than that, Pirelli will be doing its utmost to avoid the farrago that occurred at last year's British GP when four drivers had blow-outs in the race. There had been talk of making cars come in for at least two pitstops but the teams rejected this.

This year's cars will have lower noses, with their tip no more than 185mm from the ground, down from 550mm in 2012, and the ugly stepped nose solution used by some teams has been banned. Another aerodynamic change is that exhausts must exit angled upwards towards the rear wing rather than downwards towards the diffuser as before.

To demonstrate environmental credentials, fuel flow has been restricted to 100kg per hour above 10,500rpm. Also, each driver will be permitted to use only five engines during the season.

One rule change that upset some of the drivers was the weight limit. This might be seen as surprising, as it's been raised, so that each car must weigh at least 690kg, including the driver, up 48kg on 2013's minimum. However, the new power units and energy recovery systems are expected to take up all of that and more, thus encouraging teams to favour lighter drivers. Mark Webber said that he reckoned teams would only want drivers of 65kg or less. Button said, "If a driver is 5kg over the desired weight, that is 0.2s per lap and it would basically be the end of the year." Nico Hulkenberg, at

74kg, was thought to have lost out on drives at both Ferrari and McLaren for this very reason.

A major gain is that rookie drivers will get track time, with an extra set of tyres allocated for use in the first half hour on Friday, which will also encourage teams to get their cars out onto the track. This will not only help the teams assess them, but will enable them to gather more data towards their qualifying and race set-ups.

Among the drivers, there's a new face at Red Bull Racing, with Daniel Ricciardo stepping up from Toro Rosso to replace Mark Webber. And Ferrari have replaced Felipe Massa with Kimi Raikkonen as Alonso's partner, thus making it a team of World Champions. Mercedes keeps the same drivers, with Lewis Hamilton and Nico Rosberg sure to feature strongly. For Lotus, the choice of drivers following Raikkonen's defection was always going to involve what budget the financially straitened team could bring in, with Romain Grosjean allowed to continue his progress and Pastor Maldonado paying for the privilege of joining him rather than the team's preferred choice of Nico Hulkenberg. The team with the most to do is McLaren. While Button was kept on despite being frustrated by a less than competitive car, Sergio Perez failed to impress and so Kevin Magnussen has taken over.

The others - Force India, Scuderia Toro Rosso, Sauber, Williams, Marussia and Caterham - will simply hope that they have found a performance gain to move them up the table.

RED BULL RACING

Another year, another pair of F1 titles seems to be Red Bull Racing's way, having secured four on the trot. You would have to expect more of the same in 2014, but perhaps one of the other teams might adapt to the new rules better. Perhaps.

There can be no doubting that Red Bull Racing, particularly with Sebastian Vettel at the wheel, will be the act to beat in 2014.

Red Bull Racing only scored its first win in 2009 but seems to have been around forever. Historians will of course point out that it won one back in 1999, when it was Stewart GP, but the team today is a very different entity.

The key is Adrian Newey, the ace designer who first wrought his magic with Williams and McLaren before being encouraged to lead the team from Milton Keynes to championship glory.

Yes, there are new aerodynamic rules to entertain him this year, but rule changes actually offer him more of a chance rather than less to steal a march on his rivals. Then, of course, the team has Sebastian Vettel, whose passion for winning shows no sign of diminishing, even after four drivers' titles in succession. Indeed, he showed extra determination last year when ignoring team orders to deny team-mate Mark Webber victory in Malaysia. It wasn't an edifying moment, but it removed any doubt that Vettel grows horns when he puts his helmet on, just as his compatriot Michael

Schumacher did. Maybe it's what happens when you win multiple world titles.

There will be no Webber this year, though, the Australian having headed to the FIA World Endurance Championship with Porsche after seven years with the team. His replacement, Daniel Ricciardo, won a battle with his Scuderia Toro Rosso team-

KEY MOMENTS AND KEY PEOPLE

CHRISTIAN HORNER
One of the few F1 team principals who have raced, Christian reached Formula 3000 in 1997, running with his own team, Arden Motorsport. After a second year in which he failed to score a point while Juan Pablo Montoya raced to the title for rivals Super Nova, he then concentrated on managing the team. By 2002, Arden was the top team, with Bjorn Wirdheim becoming its first champion in 2003 before Vitantonio Liuzzi cleaned up in 2004. When Red Bull Racing was formed in 2005, Christian was chosen to be team principal.

GOLDEN YEAR: 2011
After landing its first constructors' title in 2010, Red Bull Racing was all but untouchable in 2011, when Sebastian Vettel and Mark Webber won 12 of the 19 rounds. The season was defined by Vettel dominating qualifying then simply staying in front – his biggest win was by 22s at the opening round in Australia, the smallest just 0.630s from Lewis Hamilton's McLaren in the Spanish GP. The team's eventual margin over runners-up McLaren was 153 points.

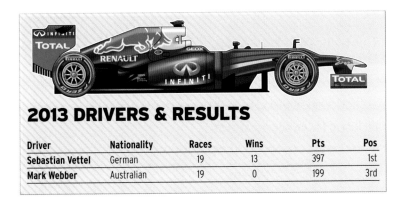

2013 DRIVERS & RESULTS

Driver	Nationality	Races	Wins	Pts	Pos
Sebastian Vettel	German	19	13	397	1st
Mark Webber	Australian	19	0	199	3rd

FOR THE RECORD

Country of origin:	England
Team base:	Milton Keynes, England
Telephone:	(44) 01908 279700
Website:	www.redbullracing.com
Active in Formula One:	From 1997 (as Stewart until 2000, then as Jaguar Racing until 2004)
Grands Prix contested:	300
Wins:	48
Pole positions:	58
Fastest laps:	41

THE TEAM

Chairman:	Dietrich Mateschitz
Team principal:	Christian Horner
Chief technical officer:	Adrian Newey
Technical coordinator:	Pierre Wache
Chief designer:	Rob Marshall
Head of engineering:	Paul Monaghan
Chief engineer:	Mark Ellis
Team manager:	Jonathan Wheatley
Test driver:	TBA
Chassis:	Red Bull RB10
Engine:	Renault V6
Tyres:	Pirelli

mate Jean-Eric Vergne to land the drive, and knows that he will have his work cut out in trying to take on undisputed team leader Vettel, a task that eventually overcame his compatriot. He's told the media that he's a team player but many insiders believe he will try to take the battle to Vettel as well. The team management has assured him that he has equal status with Vettel, but we will have to wait and see on that.

Design wise, Newey has Rob Marshall and Paul Monaghan working alongside him as chief designer and head of engineering respectively to create another car that will satisfy Red Bull magnate Dietrich Mateschitz's investment and ambition. With this stability on the design side, Red Bull Racing seems set fair for another year of extending its records. Such are the prospects that it really does seem a very long time since the dark years when this team attended grands prix as Jaguar Racing between 2001 and 2004, achieving little. The transformation has been both remarkable and complete. Add to this the fact that it controls its own training arm, Scuderia Toro Rosso, and it's easy to see why other teams now cast such envious glances in its direction, especially as other teams have limited options in bringing on their prospective stars of the future.

One thing that the team will very much want to avoid in 2014 is the swirling of rumours after Vettel's dominant performance in last year's Singapore GP that their cars were using some form of traction control, and thus running illegally. Their response was to deny that they would be so stupid, but also to reveal that they had been working on a complex engine mapping system that helped to drop the Renault V8 engine to running on just four cylinders if required to achieve enhanced traction. Yet, with Vettel's game rising inexorably as Red Bull grew to understand last year's tyres, it hardly seemed to be something that they needed to risk.

Red Bull Racing is still the one to beat.

"Daniel is up against one of the [most] successful drivers of all time, but he has the character to deal with that. And, most fundamentally, he has tremendous speed."
Christian Horner

This is the sight the other teams fear – Adrian Newey deep in thought.

SEBASTIAN VETTEL

Last year's target was for Sebastian to make it four world titles in a row. This year's is to match Michael Schumacher's feat and make it five ... It really appears to be that simple, and it would surely take a revolution for this to be denied.

When Sebastian qualified on pole for the first two of last year's grands prix, his rivals must have thought, "Here we go again." Yet, with teams taking time to comprehend the longevity of Pirelli's tyre compounds, he wasn't able to escape, as not only Fernando Alonso and Kimi Raikkonen but the Mercedes drivers also notched up wins. But then it happened, and Sebastian moved into a class of his own again and his one-finger-raised salute in parc fermé became a regular feature again.

The big question is whether anyone will be able to topple him. It happens to even the greatest, eventually, as we saw in 2005 when Alonso ended Michael Schumacher's run. There are always young guns who reckon that they could topple the driver of the moment, if only they had the right equipment. And this is the point, as Sebastian has Adrian Newey on his side, the man who has consistently produced super-competitive cars. Schumacher didn't have that advantage, and that is why he was toppled, rather than because of any loss of talent. It makes bleak reading for his rivals, but it's very hard to see anyone finding a

Sebastian's ready smile conceals an inner drive and an uncompromising will to win.

way of keeping Sebastian from making it five drivers' titles in a row in 2014.

Seb didn't enjoy being booed on the podium, most notably at Monza after he had won the Italian GP, and also in Singapore,

but his smiling countenance conceals an almost total self-belief backed up by sheer determination and a strong work ethic.

TRACK NOTES

Nationality:	GERMAN
Born:	3 JULY 1987, HEPPENHEIM, GERMANY
Website:	www.sebastianvettel.de
Teams:	BMW SAUBER 2007, TORO ROSSO 2007-08, RED BULL RACING 2009-14

CAREER RECORD

First Grand Prix:	2007 UNITED STATES GP
Grand Prix starts:	120
Grand Prix wins:	39

2008 Italian GP, 2009 Chinese GP, British GP, Japanese GP, Abu Dhabi GP, 2010 Malaysian GP, European GP, Japanese GP, Brazilian GP, Abu Dhabi GP, 2011 Australian GP, Malaysian GP, Turkish GP, Spanish GP, Monaco GP, European GP, Belgian GP, Italian GP, Singapore GP, Korean GP, Indian GP, 2012 Bahrain GP, Singapore GP, Japanese GP, Korean GP, Indian GP, 2013 Malaysian GP, Bahrain GP, Canadian GP, German GP, Belgian GP, Italian GP, Singapore GP, Korean GP, Japanese GP, Indian GP, Abu Dhabi GP, United States GP, Brazilian GP

Poles:	45
Fastest laps:	22
Points:	1,451
Honours:	2010, 2011, 2012 & 2013 FORMULA ONE WORLD CHAMPION, 2006 EUROPEAN FORMULA 3 RUNNER-UP, 2004 GERMAN FORMULA BMW CHAMPION, 2003 GERMAN FORMULA BMW RUNNER-UP, 2001 EUROPEAN & GERMAN JUNIOR KART CHAMPION

MAKING IT LOOK SO EASY

Like so many of his Formula One rivals, Sebastian was a national karting champion. Then, even before he had turned 16, he advanced to Germany's entry-level Formula BMW ADAC series and was runner-up in that. At the second time of asking, in 2003, he blitzed the opposition, winning 18 of the 20 races. With Red Bull backing, Sebastian advanced to Formula Three and was top rookie in the European series. He returned in 2006, but was kept in second place by Paul di Resta. In 2007 Sebastian raced the more powerful Renault World Series cars, and he was leading the championship when he landed his F1 break after Robert Kubica was injured in the Canadian GP, leaving an opening at BMW Sauber. He finished eighth on his debut at Indianapolis and returned later in the season with Scuderia Toro Rosso, finishing fourth in China. In 2008, he won the Italian GP and this earned him promotion to Red Bull Racing. Runner-up overall to Brawn GP's Jenson Button in 2009, he then won the next four titles, breaking records on his way.

DANIEL RICCIARDO

This year will be the first taste of the absolute big time for Daniel, and he knows that he must hit the ground running if he is to do enough to convince Red Bull Racing that he could be Sebastian Vettel's long-term replacement.

Daniel knows that by winning promotion to Red Bull Racing he has landed one of the most coveted drives in Formula One. He knows too that Sebastian Vettel has the team centred around him in a relationship that clearly works exceedingly well, as shown by his and the team's four consecutive drivers' and constructors' titles. However, Daniel isn't a driver short on ambition or determination, a fact sometimes masked by his ever-present smile, and he is definitely preparing himself to take a tilt at toppling the German.

This could be viewed as idle talk, but it isn't. Sure, the Australian hasn't finished a grand prix in higher than seventh place, but some of his qualifying runs for Scuderia Toro Rosso over the past two years have been remarkable, showing that the raw speed is there.

Also, Red Bull team principal Christian Horner was very impressed when he gave Daniel a test last summer. Perhaps even more important than that, Daniel was handpicked to go on to Red Bull's junior driver programme by Red Bull's driver

Daniel's excellence in qualifying is what convinced Red Bull Racing of his potential.

advisor Helmut Marko, allowing him a connection that Mark Webber never had, so perhaps the famously tough Austrian will view him more favourably and allow him equipment that is closer

to being equal with Vettel's than Webber sometimes felt that he was getting.

"At this point, I haven't got close to a podium but, if I've got the material under me, I can pull it off," offered Daniel. "I'm not going to know until testing how I go against Seb, but for now that's what I'm thinking."

Podium finishes at the very least will be what he's aiming for. If one of them sees him scaling the top step of the podium, then he really will have been rewarded for a journey that began back in 2007 when he left home aged 17 to race in Europe.

TRACK NOTES

Nationality:	AUSTRALIAN
Born:	1 JULY 1989, PERTH, AUSTRALIA
Website:	www.danielricciardo.com
Teams:	HRT 2011, TORO ROSSO 2012-13, RED BULL RACING 2014

CAREER RECORD	
First Grand Prix:	2011 BRITISH GP
Grand Prix starts:	50
Grand Prix wins:	0
	(best result: 7th, 2013 Chinese GP & Italian GP)
Poles:	0
Fastest laps:	0
Points:	30
Honours:	2010 FORMULA RENAULT 3.5 RUNNER-UP, 2009 BRITISH FORMULA THREE CHAMPION, 2008 EUROPEAN FORMULA RENAULT RUNNER-UP & WESTERN EUROPEAN FORMULA RENAULT CHAMPION

CLIMBING THE LADDER TO THE TOP

Daniel has achieved a feat that very few fellow Red Bull-backed young drivers have done: made it to a race seat with Red Bull Racing. Plenty have been supported through the ranks, a smaller number have been promoted to Formula One with Red Bull's feeder team, Scuderia Toro Rosso. But he's a real rarity in then being considered good enough to move up to Red Bull Racing. Daniel's career in cars started in Formula Ford in Australia in 2005, and he then moved on to Formula BMW in 2006, racing in the Asian series. Relocating to Europe in 2007, he raced in Formula Renault, going on to land Red Bull backing for 2008 and then become runner-up in the European series. Joining Carlin Motorsport, Daniel won the British Formula Three crown in 2009. Formula Renault 3.5 was next, and in that he was runner-up in 2010. He stayed on for a second year, but then leapt at the chance to make his F1 debut with HRT when Narain Karthikeyan was dropped mid-season. He moved to Toro Rosso in 2012.

MERCEDES AMG PETRONAS

Last year was a season full of promise but this front-running team will have to wait to find out whether their ever-increasing collection of technical brains will produce a championship-winning car for Lewis Hamilton and Nico Rosberg in 2014.

Lewis Hamilton and Nico Rosberg mounted an increasingly strong campaign through 2013 and have high hopes they'll shine with the new rules.

Anyone examining the statistics for last year's World Championship will spot a pattern: pole to Mercedes AMG Petronas, then victory to Red Bull Racing or occasionally to Ferrari, as the Mercedes duo of Lewis Hamilton and Nico Rosberg found themselves without the pace to stay in front as their tyres became worn. It was a matter of frustration for all concerned. There were wins, starting with Rosberg's in Monaco, but then Red Bull became ever stronger through the second half of the season, and it became clear that this ambitious team still had some way to go if it wanted to move back to the top of the pile, a position that it has occupied only once before, when racing as Brawn GP in 2009.

So, you can guess what was being focused on in particular by the Mercedes design team through last summer as they started on this year's new car. Of course, a rule-enforced change to the aerodynamic package and the replacement of 2.4-litre V8s with 1.6-litre turbocharged units may well work in their favour, but the proof of this will only emerge in the final pre-season tests or perhaps only across the first few grands prix as the teams discover whether their cars work on the latest Pirelli tyre compounds or not.

The key signing for the modern-day Silver Arrows is former McLaren technical director Paddy Lowe, a designer with a very innovative mind who will take over the team's technical

KEY MOMENTS AND KEY PEOPLE

NIKI LAUDA
Anyone who watched the film *Rush* will appreciate how Niki galvanized Ferrari in the 1970s and turned it back into a championship-winning team. Since then, he retired from racing in 1979, built up an airline, returned to Formula One in 1982, collecting a third drivers' title in 1984 with McLaren, then retired again. He returned to F1 in 2001 to run Jaguar Racing, then in 2003 formed another airline. Niki's fourth stint in F1 began in 2012, when Mercedes GP Petronas harnessed his experience as a non-executive chairman.

GOLDEN YEAR: 2013
This team that started its life as BAR in 1999, became Honda Racing in 2006 and Brawn GP in 2009, then assumed its current identity in 2010 has been advancing each year. Even with Michael Schumacher brought back to propel it to glory, victory eluded it until Nico Rosberg triumphed in China in 2012. However, strong regular poles followed in 2013, and these were augmented by a trio of wins as Mercedes became the best of the rest, after Red Bull Racing.

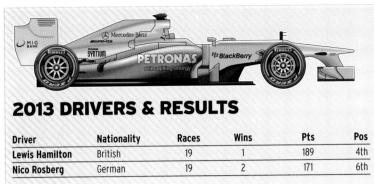

2013 DRIVERS & RESULTS

Driver	Nationality	Races	Wins	Pts	Pos
Lewis Hamilton	British	19	1	189	4th
Nico Rosberg	German	19	2	171	6th

FOR THE RECORD

Country of origin:	England
Team base:	Brackley, England
Telephone:	(44) 01280 844000
Website:	www.mercedes-amg-f1.com
Active in Formula One:	As BAR 1999-2005; Honda Racing 2006-08; Brawn GP 2009
Grands Prix contested:	265
Wins:	13
Pole positions:	17
Fastest laps:	7

THE TEAM

Non-executive chairman:	Niki Lauda
Executive director, business:	Toto Wolff
Executive director, technical:	Paddy Lowe
Technical director:	Bob Bell
Technology director:	Geoff Willis
Engineering director:	Aldo Costa
Head of aerodynamics:	Mike Elliott
Chief designer:	John Owen
Chief engineer:	Russell Cooley
Chief race engineer:	Andrew Shovlin
Sporting director:	Ron Meadows
Test driver:	Sam Bird
Chassis:	Mercedes F1 W05
Engine:	Mercedes V6
Tyres:	Pirelli

attack from Ross Brawn who stood down last November. What remains to be seen is how well his talents fit together with those of Mercedes' established technical stars Bob Bell, Geoff Willis, Aldo Costa and John Owen.

After a spell of "gardening leave", Lowe was itching to get started, saying, "Mercedes produced probably the fastest car of 2013, while the technical challenge of the new regulations gives us the opportunity to maximize the synergies available to a works manufacturer. That's a challenge I'm relishing. I've worked closely with Mercedes for almost 20 years and deeply admire the company's phenomenal commitment to F1."

One thing proved conclusively last year was just how good Rosberg is. During his three years partnering Michael Schumacher, he came out ahead, so people said that the seven-time World Champion must have lost his edge. It was only last year, when he was paired with Hamilton, and raced just as fast and hard, that fans found out just how quick he is and, at the same time, how Schumacher had lost very little of his speed after all.

It's not just in the technical department that there have been changes, with former chief executive officer Nick Fry standing down last April to work on a consultancy basis with the team's commercial operations. In his place, Toto Wolff was appointed as executive director, joining from Williams.

An even bigger name drafted in to help guide the team to greater things is none other than three-time World Champion Niki Lauda, who was appointed last year as non-executive director, giving him the sort of overseeing role in which he can bring his vast experience to bear. He can be blunt, but he's seldom anything other than on the money when it comes to pinpointing what's standing between a team and success, as witnessed by those who saw him turn Ferrari around when he became lead driver in 1974.

"To deliver in this time of rule changes, a successful team needs strength in depth. Paddy Lowe's arrival will further strengthen our organization and puts us in a strong position for the future."
Ross Brawn

Out with the old and in with the new: Toto Wolff (left) chats to Niki Lauda.

LEWIS HAMILTON

Lewis had an impressive first season with Mercedes AMG Petronas, but he will be desperate for a car good enough to take the fight to Red Bull Racing and Sebastian Vettel over race distance, not just in qualifying.

Last year was one in which the truly fast guys shone. It was former World Champions Fernando Alonso, Kimi Raikkonen and Lewis who, more often than not, joined runaway 2013 champion Sebastian Vettel on the podium.

In the early part of the season, though, it was Nico Rosberg leading the way for Mercedes, collecting pole positions galore and then that victory at Monaco. Then it was Lewis's turn to strike and he looked back to his best form. Pole for four consecutive grands prix - Silverstone, the Nurburgring, the Hungaroring and Spa-Francorchamps - showed that he had lost none of his one-lap speed. This wasn't often rewarded in the races, though, as the Mercedes F1 W04 was hard on its tyres, but progress was made and Lewis came out ahead to win in Hungary, becoming a rare interruption in Red Bull Racing's streak.

The other good thing was that Lewis appeared to be competing in a far happier frame of mind than he had in 2012. Then he had seemed to be overwrought, emotional matters making him lose the

Lewis was hard on himself in 2013, but is determined to get a grip on this year's car.

ultimate focus that is required if any driver is going to succeed in this most exacting of sports.

The battle this year will be again first and foremost to outscore his team-mate, but if the team's brains trust led by the incoming Paddy Lowe can come up with the goods, then Lewis might be able to take a shot at the second World Championship title that his talent so clearly merits.

TRACK NOTES

Nationality:	BRITISH
Born: 7 JANUARY 1985, STEVENAGE, ENGLAND	
Website:	www.lewishamilton.com
Teams: McLAREN 2007-12, MERCEDES 2013-14	

CAREER RECORD

First Grand Prix:	2007 AUSTRALIAN GP
Grand Prix starts:	129
Grand Prix wins:	22

2007 Canadian GP, United States GP, Hungarian GP, Japanese GP, 2008 Australian GP, Monaco GP, British GP, German GP, Chinese GP, 2009 Hungarian GP, Singapore GP, 2010 Turkish GP, Canadian GP, Belgian GP, 2011 Chinese GP, German GP, Abu Dhabi GP, 2012 Canadian GP, Hungarian GP, Italian GP, United States GP, 2013 Hungarian GP

Poles:	31
Fastest laps:	13
Points:	1102
Honours:	2008 FORMULA ONE WORLD CHAMPION, 2007 FORMULA ONE RUNNER-UP, 2006 GP2 CHAMPION, 2005 EUROPEAN FORMULA THREE CHAMPION, 2003 BRITISH FORMULA RENAULT CHAMPION, 2000 WORLD KART CUP CHAMPION & EUROPEAN FORMULA A KART CHAMPION, 1999 ITALIAN INTERCONTINENTAL A KART CHAMPION, 1996 McLAREN MERCEDES CHAMPION OF THE FUTURE, 1995 BRITISH CADET KARTING CHAMPION

SUCCEEDING FOR HIS BACKERS

Lewis's family didn't have the money to take him into car racing, with his father Anthony having to hold down three jobs just to finance his kart racing. However, his abundant skill was clear for all to see, and a cheeky comment to McLaren chief Ron Dennis at an awards dinner landed him the backing that he needed. So, as soon as he was old enough, he moved up to cars, starting in Formula Renault, and he was British champion in 2003 at his second attempt. In 2005 he added the European Formula Three crown, with Adrian Sutil runner-up and Sebastian Vettel back in fifth overall. It then took him just one year to become GP2 champion, with ART Grand Prix, and so McLaren found a seat for its highly rated protégé. Amazingly, he came up just one point short of being a rookie World Champion, pipped by Ferrari's Kimi Raikkonen, before edging out Felipe Massa by a similar margin to take the crown a year later. Feeling that he had achieved what he could at McLaren, Lewis moved on to Mercedes for 2013.

NICO ROSBERG

Last year was Nico's best to date, and his form both in qualifying and in the races proved that he is one of Formula One's top drivers. He must now be hoping that Mercedes has kept up its development of this year's new generation of cars.

Being the son of a World Champion gives you a hard act to follow, particularly if your father was as rumbustious as Keke was, yet Nico has been proving himself to be right up there with the best of his era. When he partnered Lewis Hamilton in their karting days, it was felt somewhat inevitably that Hamilton was the rising star, Nico the wealthy also-ran. Yet, this has proved to be unfair as Nico was a championship winner in his first year out of karts, racing in the Formula BMW ADAC Championship, then shone in Formula Three and then won the title in GP2 – Formula One's immediate feeder formula – in only his fourth year of car racing.

After serving his apprenticeship with Williams, even setting the race's fastest lap on his debut, he moved to Mercedes for 2010, but due to the Williams team's declining form, many had forgotten about Nico's speed and so expected the returning Michael Schumacher – a seven-time World Champion no less – to dominate him. History relates, though, that it was Nico and not Michael who set the pace and landed the results.

Nico drove really well in 2013, but will be praying the Mercedes won't fade in races.

Being paired with Hamilton last year further bolstered Nico's reputation, and winning for Mercedes at Monaco, the hometown of his childhood, had extra emotional value. That he never put a wheel wrong added to his family's delight. He also won at the British GP, but that triumph at Silverstone was destined to go first to Hamilton (until he suffered tyre failure), then to Vettel (until his gearbox broke).

It's true that Hamilton came on strong through the year and ended up marginally ahead, but how they rate against each other this year will depend how they adapt to the new car and all the new regulations. Friends since childhood, they know each other well and have a respect for each other that should ensure that there's a degree of harmony in the team seldom enjoyed by outfits with two chargers in their line-up.

TRACK NOTES

Nationality:	GERMAN
Born:	27 JUNE 1985, WIESBADEN, GERMANY
Website:	www.nicorosberg.com
Teams:	WILLIAMS 2006-09,
	MERCEDES 2010-14

CAREER RECORD	
First Grand Prix:	2006 BAHRAIN GP
Grand Prix starts:	147
Grand Prix wins:	3
2012 Chinese GP, 2013 Monaco GP, British GP	
Poles:	4
Fastest laps:	4
Points:	570.5
Honours:	2005 GP2 CHAMPION,
	2003 EUROPEAN FORMULA THREE ROOKIE
	RUNNER-UP, 2002 FORMULA BMW ADAC
	CHAMPION, 2000 EUROPEAN FORMULA A
	KART RUNNER-UP

FORGING HIS OWN NAME IN F1

Nico raced karts as a child, and was runner-up in the European Formula A Kart Championship in 2000 when he was 15. At this point in his career, he was outperformed by his team-mate Lewis Hamilton, yet he immediately proved his credentials when he moved into car racing by dominating the 2002 Formula BMW ADAC series. Nico was then top rookie in European Formula Three in 2003. Where he really showed that he might be more than a famous surname was when he advanced to GP2 after two years of F3 and won the title at his first attempt, racing for ART Grand Prix. So, it wasn't a case of Williams picking Nico for 2006 simply because his father had won the 1982 F1 drivers' title for the team, but because he was fast. When he set the fastest lap for the first race, it was clear that he was a talent, but his next three years were hard as Williams became less competitive, making his jump to Mercedes in 2010 a good move, where he impressed people by being more than a match for illustrious team-mate Michael Schumacher.

Lewis Hamilton had a season in which he didn't always understand his Mercedes, but still displayed some flashes of natural speed, winning once in Hungary.

SCUDERIA FERRARI

In bringing Kimi Raikkonen back into the fold, Ferrari has made a statement that Fernando Alonso won't have everything his own way in 2014. Watching how well these World Champions work together is going to be very interesting.

Fernando Alonso felt that his car wasn't ever fast enough to tackle the Red Bulls in 2013 so will be hoping that the rule changes help Ferrari.

There were more fireworks in the Ferrari pit garage last year than there were for the Italian team out on the track. What isn't a matter for debate is that Red Bull Racing gave Sebastian Vettel a better car in which to go racing. Also, there can be no quibbles that the German had a better time of things than Fernando Alonso did, with the Spaniard undoubtedly doing a stunning job in a car that was never the class of the field.

Ferrari drivers of old felt that he was unwise to air his criticisms so publicly, and Ferrari responded by signing Kimi Raikkonen. It's not known whether this was because they worried that the Spanish ace would jump ship, perhaps to McLaren, or because they truly believed that they could finally run two number one drivers after decades of making one very much secondary to the other. Think back to Michael Schumacher's days and the way that his then team-mate Rubens Barrichello would only win races towards the end of the year, after Michael had clinched another title. Think of how Barrichello was

instructed to back right off to let Schumacher through to win in Austria in 2002 or of how Felipe Massa had to perform a similar service to let Alonso past at Hockenheim in 2010.

These weren't instances that suggest that the team is happy simply to let its drivers race, but it is difficult to imagine Raikkonen being happy to play second fiddle. Massa was

KEY MOMENTS AND KEY PEOPLE

LUCA DI MONTEZEMOLO
Born into the Agnelli family that owns Fiat, and thus Ferrari from 1969, Luca was sent to work for Enzo Ferrari in 1973, then put in charge of the day-to-day running of the F1 team in 1974. Niki Lauda helped it claim three titles in a row from 1975. In 1977, he was put in charge of the Fiat empire. He also oversaw Italy's America's Cup yachting challenge and Italy's football World Cup in 1990. On his watch, Ferrari returned to title-winning form with Michael Schumacher in 2000.

GOLDEN YEAR: 2002
The early 1952 and 1953 seasons were almost all Ferrari, as was 1961; then Niki Lauda came out on top in 1975 and 1977, and Jody Scheckter in 1979. However, Ferrari went to sleep and it took Michael Schumacher's speed and drive to put the team back on top of the pile. He did this in 2000 and went on to win the title each year until 2004, but the zenith was the 2002 season, when he won 11 of the 17 rounds, with Rubens Barrichello adding four more.

2013 DRIVERS & RESULTS

Driver	Nationality	Races	Wins	Pts	Pos
Fernando Alonso	Spanish	19	2	242	2nd
Felipe Massa	Brazilian	19	0	112	8th

FOR THE RECORD

Country of origin:	Italy
Team base:	Maranello, Italy
Telephone:	(39) 536 949111
Website:	www.ferrari.com
Active in Formula One:	From 1950
Grands Prix contested:	851
Wins:	219
Pole positions:	207
Fastest laps:	225

THE TEAM

President:	Luca di Montezemolo
Chief executive officer:	Amedeo Felisa
Team principal:	Stefano Domenicali
Technical director:	James Allison
Chassis director:	Pat Fry
Production director:	Corrado Lanzone
Engine & electronics director:	Luca Marmorini
Chief designer:	Nikolas Tombazis
Chief aerodynamicist:	Dirk de Beer
Sporting director:	Massimo Rivola
Chief engineer:	Steve Clark
Test drivers:	Pedro de la Rosa & Marc Gene
Chassis:	Ferrari F148
Engine:	Ferrari V6
Tyres:	Pirelli

suitably acquiescent over the years before being edged out at the end of last season, but Raikkonen has shown before, famously, how he doesn't respond well to mid-race suggestions over his radio ... So, drama is all but guaranteed and you can be sure that Formula One supremo Bernie Ecclestone will be rubbing his hands with glee at the soap opera that is to unfold.

So, Ferrari has two of the best drivers, both aching for wins, and the onus is now on the team to provide them cars that are capable of achieving them, otherwise their undoubted skills will be going to waste.

The crux for Ferrari this year is to produce a car that can match or beat the Red Bull. Perhaps there's more of a chance of this happening with the major rule changes for this year, but the quality of the cars that Adrian Newey and his design crew have been turning out for Red Bull Racing over the past four years has been exceptional and suggests that he will probably do it again. How the Ferrari behaves on its tyres is a critical matter, with Alonso blaming an inability to get last year's car to use its rubber well for the team's relative loss of form after Pirelli introduced a new range of tyres midway through 2013. Chief designer Nikolas

Tombazis debated whether that was indeed the reason why the Red Bull pulled further ahead, and suggested that it was more likely due to the team's wind tunnel technology lagging behind its rivals', especially in terms of its flow quality. Fortunately for the tifosi, Ferrari updated its wind tunnel last year and better results are expected from it for 2014.

Stefano Domenicali remains at the helm as the one who has to answer to Luca di Montezemolo, but there have been changes beneath him, and the team has gained even more of a British influence with the arrival last autumn of James Allison from Lotus to be technical director and thus work with fellow Briton Pat Fry, who has been chassis director since joining from McLaren in 2011.

"Last year, our wind tunnel technology was a weak point ... so we couldn't do that many runs and experiments per day, which was a bit of a drawback."
Nikolas Tombazis

Stefano Domenicali's famous good nature may be tested by the Alonso-Raikkonen combination.

Chasing after Sebastian Vettel's Red Bull last year was a constant and dispiriting challenge for Fernando, and it looks as though his angry outbursts about how uncompetitive his Ferrari was may have compromised his standing with the team.

This year Fernando is going to find out what it's like with Ferrari attempting to run two drivers on an equal footing as the acquiescent Felipe Massa has been replaced by the mercurial Kimi Raikkonen.

There were some drives of incredible endeavour last year, showing that this two-time World Champion is a force to be reckoned with even when not armed with the best equipment available. Fernando finished higher in races than many of his rivals in superior cars, which is the mark of a true champion. Indeed, his run of three second-place finishes in a row, at Spa-Francorchamps, Monza and on Singapore's Marina Bay street circuit, impressed even more than his early-season victories at Shanghai and Barcelona, as the Ferrari F138's relative level of performance had fallen by then.

What was clearly a matter of frustration for Fernando, though, was that the team's upgrades through the season simply didn't yield the sort of performance gains as those introduced by Red Bull Racing and Mercedes. His response was one that certainly harmed his relationship with

Fernando will be kept on his toes by Kimi but will still deliver if the car is good.

Ferrari, especially as far as company president Luca di Montezemolo was concerned, and it prompted former Ferrari F1 race winner Jean Alesi to comment that it had been rash of Fernando to complain

about Ferrari's F1 cars in public. Hopefully he won't have reason to speak out again in 2014 and the new-look Ferrari will be a competitive proposition.

TRACK NOTES

Nationality:	SPANISH
Born:	29 JULY 1981, OVIEDO, SPAIN
Website:	www.fernandoalonso.com
Teams:	MINARDI 2001, RENAULT
	2003–06, McLAREN 2007, RENAULT 2008–09,
	FERRARI 2010–14

CAREER RECORD

First Grand Prix:	2001 AUSTRALIAN GP
Grand Prix starts:	217
Grand Prix wins:	32

2003 Hungarian GP, 2005 Malaysian GP, Bahrain GP, San Marino GP, European GP, French GP, German GP, Chinese GP, 2006 Bahrain GP, Australian GP, Spanish GP, Monaco GP, British GP, Canadian GP, Japanese GP, 2007 Malaysian GP, Monaco GP, European GP, Italian GP, 2008 Singapore GP, Japanese GP, 2010 Australian GP, German GP, Italian GP, Singapore GP, Korean GP, 2011 British GP, 2012 Malaysian GP, European GP, German GP, 2013 Chinese GP, Spanish GP

Poles:	22
Fastest laps:	21
Points:	1,606
Honours:	2005 & 2006 FORMULA ONE

WORLD CHAMPION, 2010 & 2012 FORMULA ONE RUNNER-UP, 1999 FORMULA NISSAN CHAMPION, 1997 ITALIAN & SPANISH KART CHAMPION, 1996 WORLD & SPANISH KART CHAMPION, 1994 & 1995 SPANISH JUNIOR KART CHAMPION

MAKING IT ALL LOOK SO EASY

A few drivers stand out from the moment that they start racing, but many fall by the wayside and a far smaller number carry that potential all the way through to Formula One. Often they grow too big or too poorly funded, or sometimes someone even quicker comes along. Fernando was one of the very few who made himself stand out and has never stopped doing so. World Kart Champion in 1996, he then had to bide his time, winning more titles, until he was old enough to graduate to cars in 1999. He not only skipped formulae but won the Formula Nissan title. Formula 3000 was next, and he took a dominant win at Spa-Francorchamps to show that he was ready for F1. Minardi signed him for 2001 and, after spending 2002 as Renault's test driver, he won for the team in Hungary in 2003. World Champion for Renault in 2005 and 2006, he endured a mixed year with McLaren before returning to Renault. He has been Ferrari's lead driver since 2010, but is still waiting for a car to help him to another title.

KIMI RAIKKONEN

When Ferrari paid Kimi off to leave the team at the end of 2009 so that he could go rallying, no one would have predicted that he'd ever drive for them again, yet here he is, brought back to push Fernando Alonso and help Ferrari to score more points.

Actually, that is the burning question: was Kimi brought back chiefly to let Fernando know that he wasn't running the team or to ensure that both Ferraris scored points more frequently to help the team in the constructors' championship? Or both?

Whatever the answer, the Flying Finn is back for a second spell with the team from Maranello. His first spell with Ferrari yielded a drivers' championship in 2007, a title that had been denied him at McLaren, ironically just ahead of both McLaren drivers, one of whom was Alonso. Yet, by 2009, his form was on the wane and many felt that he had lost interest as he trailed the Red Bull driver, the Brawn GP drivers and McLaren's Lewis Hamilton. Ferrari wanted new blood and so they dipped into their not inconsequential budget and bought him out of his contract to make the opening into which they wanted to slot Alonso.

Now that he's back for a second stint, one thing that was made plain by his performances with Lotus over the past two campaigns is that the taste for winning has returned, perhaps fired by

Kimi's return to Maranello certainly provides an interesting twist for 2014.

not achieving what he had hoped with Citroen in the World Rally Championship. He still loathes any duties other than in the cockpit, most notably anything that involves a TV camera or a microphone. In

fact, Kimi has made it plain that he doesn't even welcome any communication from the pitwall, but he is back to his best behind the wheel, scoring just as many points as his car is capable of delivering, bringing speed if not PR proficiency.

TRACK NOTES

Nationality:	FINNISH
Born:	17 OCTOBER 1979, ESPOO, FINLAND
Website:	www.kimiraikkonen.com
Teams:	SAUBER 2001, McLAREN 2002-06, FERRARI 2007-09, LOTUS 2012-13, FERRARI 2014

CAREER RECORD	
First Grand Prix:	2001 AUSTRALIAN GP
Grand Prix starts:	194
Grand Prix wins:	20
	2003 Malaysian GP, 2004 Belgian GP, 2005 Spanish GP, Monaco GP, Canadian GP, Hungarian GP, Turkish GP, Belgian GP, Japanese GP, 2007 Australian GP, French GP, British GP, Belgian GP, Chinese GP, Brazilian GP, 2008 Malaysian GP, Spanish GP, 2009 Belgian GP, 2012 Abu Dhabi GP, 2013 Australian GP
Poles:	16
Fastest laps:	39
Points:	969
Honours:	2007 FORMULA ONE WORLD CHAMPION, 2003 & 2005 FORMULA ONE RUNNER-UP, 2000 BRITISH FORMULA RENAULT CHAMPION, 1999 BRITISH FORMULA RENAULT WINTER SERIES CHAMPION, 1998 EUROPEAN SUPER A KART RUNNER-UP, FINNISH KART CHAMPION & NORDIC KART CHAMPION

»

FROM RACING TO RALLYING AND BACK

Kimi has always done things differently. He eschewed the traditional route of graduating through the junior formulae shortly after stepping up from karts. Formula Renault was enough for him, he reckoned. In his mind there was no need to bother with Formula Three and then GP2. Instead, his managers simply arranged a test with the Sauber Formula One team, who were so impressed that they signed him for the following year, 2001, after just 23 car races... To make it more impressive still, he finished in sixth place on his debut in Australia and did enough to be signed by McLaren for 2002. He was then runner-up to Michael Schumacher in 2003, then to Renault's Fernando Alonso in 2005. Kimi joined Ferrari in 2007 and stole the title from under the noses of the McLaren drivers at the Brazilian finale. But, being different, he was happy to be bought out later by Ferrari so that he could try the World Rally Championship. Ever restless, he returned to F1 in 2012 with Lotus and won the Abu Dhabi GP.

LOTUS F1 TEAM

The Lotus F1 Team put better-financed Ferrari, McLaren and Mercedes to shame last year when it produced a car that was good to race and frequently finished second only to Red Bull Racing. The trick will be to repeat this form in 2014.

Romain Grosjean turned from the team's number two into its number one during 2013 and is deservedly the team leader for the season ahead.

There continues to be a confusion of identity when discussing this team. Lotus, of course, was once a successful team that set the pace from the 1960s through to the 1970s then shone once more with Ayrton Senna in the mid-1980s. Then it went bust. Having its name used later by Tony Fernandes' team when it started life in 2010 was confusing. Having this name transferred to a third team in 2012 was more so. And matters were made even more confusing when you considered that the team now carrying the Lotus name had started life as Toleman in 1981, become Benetton in 1986, and was then run as Renault from 2002 to 2011. Not the original Renault, mind... This is why the team now known as Lotus is often called "Team Enstone", after the location in Oxfordshire where it has been based for so many decades.

Whatever the past, though, last year's form was marginally better than its excellent 2012 campaign. It started with victory in the opening round as Kimi Raikkonen won in Melbourne. Seven second-place finishes and six thirds showed just how strong their form was as the black and gold cars came home again and again ahead of the best-placed Ferrari, Mercedes and McLaren entries. What stood out, though, was that Raikkonen's and, increasingly, Romain Grosjean's form was stronger in the races than in qualifying, as both gathered large helpings of points

KEY MOMENTS AND KEY PEOPLE

ERIC BOULLIER
A popular member of the F1 paddock, Eric worked his way up by running teams for DAMS in the junior formulae, overseeing the engineering of the French outfit's attacks in GP2, A1GP and even Formula BMW, meaning that he was busy almost every weekend of the summer. At the end of 2008, just before A1GP folded, he moved across to run Gravity Sport Management, and his boss there, Gerard Lopez, took over what had been the Renault F1 team, installing Eric as its team principal for its 2010 debut. The wins began again in 2012.

GOLDEN YEAR: 1995
The wins have been starting to trickle in since the team became rebadged as Lotus for 2012, but this team from Enstone was in its absolute pomp in 1995 when it raced as Benetton, when Flavio Briatore was in charge, and it landed a supply of Renault engines. Lead driver Michael Schumacher duly followed up on his 1994 drivers' title by claiming another while Johnny Herbert added two more victories to help to give the team its first and so far only constructors' title.

2013 DRIVERS & RESULTS

Driver	Nationality	Races	Wins	Pts	Pos
Romain Grosjean	French	19	0	132	7th
Heikki Kovalainen	Finnish	2	0	0	23rd
Kimi Raikkonen	Finnish	17	1	183	5th

FOR THE RECORD

Country of origin:	England
Team base:	Enstone, England
Telephone:	(44) 01608 678000
Website:	www.lotusf1team.com
Active in Formula One:	As Toleman 1981-85; Benetton 1986-2001, Renault 2002-11
Grands Prix contested:	534
Wins:	48
Pole positions:	34
Fastest laps:	56

THE TEAM

Chairman:	Gerard Lopez
Chief executive officer:	Patrick Louis
Chief operating officer:	Thomas Mayer
Team principal:	Eric Boullier
Technical director:	Nick Chester
Operations director:	Alan Permane
Chief designer:	Martin Tolliday
Head of aerodynamics:	Nicolas Hennel de Beaupreau
Chief engineer:	Ciaron Pilbeam
Team manager:	Paul Seaby
Test driver:	TBA
Chassis:	Lotus E22
Engine:	Renault V6
Tyres:	Pirelli

almost every time that they were available. The French ace, 28 this spring, managed largely to shed his "wild man" tag during 2013. As a consequence, he finished races rather than crashing and was able to gather a useful haul of points. By the end of the year, he was performing to the very highest level, especially in his race to second place in the United States GP, and will be a worthy team leader for 2014.

Money, or the lack of it, was a problem last year for Lotus, with talk in late summer of bills not getting paid and thus employee dissatisfaction. However, one ray of light was Dubai's Emaar Properties signing a deal with the team. The company has a high profile, having built the renowned Burj Khalifa hotel and the giant Dubai Mall. As part of Emaar Properties' pursuit of global recognition, the company is pushing for Dubai to land a place on the World Championship calendar, with a street race in downtown Dubai.

There was then a move to buy the team by hedge fund manager Mansoor Ijaz. This was going to bring in the backing that would enable the team to sign Nico Hulkenberg from Sauber after some remarkable drives in the second half of last season. However, continued delays in the arrival of money from this investor led to the team turning to Pastor Maldonado as he could bring backing from PDVSA.

Team principal Eric Boullier had every reason to be delighted with not just his drivers' form last year but the team's, as it took on Ferrari, McLaren and Mercedes, all with infinitely larger budgets, and beat them all on occasion. However, technical director James Allison left and chairman Gerard Lopez must maintain a flow of money into the team's coffers or it might slide back behind its immediate rivals again. Its facilities are good enough to do the job, but you can't stand still if you want to go forward.

"We've been working on our new car in alignment with the new regulations for over two years and we are confident that we have a very good solution to all the challenges ahead."
Eric Boullier

Gerard Lopez (left) and Eric Boullier have reasons to be delighted with the team's speed.

ROMAIN GROSJEAN

Romain came of age in 2013 by eliminating the accidents that had peppered his career in 2012. Now, with Kimi Raikkonen gone to Ferrari, he must grab his opportunity to prove a worthy team leader for the Lotus F1 Team.

Drivers can be as fast as each other, but the point when they really come of age in Formula One is when they start to boss the team. This had never previously been Romain's way, especially with Kimi Raikkonen ruling the roost at Lotus. Then, late last season, there was an interesting development when Romain was angered by the Lotus team not electing to impose team orders during the Korean GP and let him move ahead of team-mate Raikkonen, who was between him and race leader Sebastian Vettel and, in Romain's mind, delaying him. Team principal Eric Boullier liked seeing this anger and declared that this was "the Romain we want".

It will take more than this incident alone to make other team bosses think that he might be someone who could lead their attack some day, but it was very much a step in the right direction. With Raikkonen having already announced that he was heading off to Ferrari for 2014 when this happened, it was seen as a sign that perhaps he'd already started to assume the role of team leader. Small wonder then that Boullier, long a supporter of Romain's,

Romain did everything he could in 2013 and this year's target must be his first F1 win.

started to talk of his charge in such a different and more positive way.

Romain didn't just fight his corner in this manner last year but also by increasing his pace to the point in the second half of the season that he was matching Raikkonen in races as well as in qualifying. He finished second behind Vettel in last year's United States GP, keeping Mark Webber back in third, and backed this up with five third-place finishes during 2013 to help him to rank seventh overall, so the speed is clearly there to take his first grand prix win, if given the right equipment.

The season ahead marks a new stage for Romain as it will be the first time that he has been a team leader, and he appeared to blossom through 2013 once it was clear that the team had put its weight behind him.

TRACK NOTES

Nationality:	FRENCH
Born:	17 APRIL 1986, GENEVA, SWITZERLAND
Website:	www.romaingrosjean.com
Teams:	RENAULT 2009, LOTUS 2012-14

CAREER RECORD	
First Grand Prix:	2009 EUROPEAN GP
Grand Prix starts:	45
Grand Prix wins:	0
(best result: 2nd, 2012 Canadian GP, 2013 United States GP)	
Poles:	0
Fastest laps:	1
Points:	228
Honours:	2011 GP2 CHAMPION & GP2 ASIA CHAMPION, 2010 AUTO GP CHAMPION, 2008 GP2 ASIA CHAMPION, 2007 FORMULA THREE EURO SERIES CHAMPION, 2005 FRENCH FORMULA RENAULT CHAMPION, 2003 SWISS FORMULA RENAULT 1600 CHAMPION

COMING BACK FOR MORE

Timing is everything in comedy and also in motor racing. Take Romain's career, for example. He had won pretty much everything that there was to win on his ascent up the greasy pole through the various junior single-seater formulae to the brink of Formula One. Then, when Nelson Piquet Jr was banned from F1 midway through 2009 for his part in race-fixing at Singapore the previous year, Romain was promoted from the Renault team's test driver role. The Renault R29 wasn't a great car, but even so he wasn't thought to have done enough to keep the ride, and so he was an F1 reject by the age of 23. Few people get a second chance but Romain bounced back and won the Auto GP title and then took the brave step of having a second spell in GP2. To achieve anything, he had to win the championship, and he duly did just that. So he had served his second apprenticeship and returned to the team that had dropped him, now under its new name, Lotus. His speed was soon plain, but a string of accidents tempered this.

PASTOR MALDONADO

After Pastor and Williams fell out at the end of their three years together, he became the key to the driver market last autumn on account of the large budget that he could bring with him – and which helped him into the second Lotus seat for 2014.

It's no exaggeration to say that Pastor had a tumultuous 2013 season, and it continued to have more lows than highs as he scored but one point, for 10th place in the Hungarian GP back at the end of July.

Pastor's drive for 2014 had become uncertain when Venezuelan president Hugo Chavez died last March and there were question marks about whether he would keep his backing from state oil company PDVSA. At this point, with the Williams team's form declining as they struggled to get the FW35 to perform, Pastor said that he had lost motivation and even that he'd rather stay at home than race an uncompetitive car in 2014.

"I don't care about being a Formula One driver," he said at the time. "I'm not here to fight [Valtteri] Bottas. He's a good driver, but he's not my objective. I want to fight with the big people. I'm here to win races and I need to do whatever it takes to be there. At Barcelona in 2012, when I had the chance to fight for a race win, I won."

One of the saddest events of 2013 occurred at the United States GP at the

Pastor has said that he feels refreshed by a change of scene after three years at Williams.

Circuit of the Americas in November when Pastor accused the team of having sabotaged his car in qualifying. Sure, the car had been way less competitive than he had hoped for through the season, but

he had simply been outpaced by rookie team-mate Bottas and he didn't like it. This effectively marked the end of their relationship and made the joy of his sole and surprising victory in the 2012 Spanish GP recede even further.

Claiming to be refreshed by the prospect of moving to Lotus to race alongside new team leader Romain Grosjean, Pastor said on signing last November, "It's a fantastic opportunity and it's no secret that I have wanted a change of scene to help push on with my F1 career, and Lotus offered me the very best chance for me to be competitive in 2014. The regulations and cars will change significantly, so it's a very good time for a fresh start."

TRACK NOTES

Nationality:	VENEZUELAN
Born:	9 MARCH 1985, MARACAY, VENEZUELA
Website:	www.pastormaldonado.com
Teams:	WILLIAMS 2011-13, LOTUS 2014

CAREER RECORD

First Grand Prix:	2011 AUSTRALIAN GP
Grand Prix starts:	58
Grand Prix wins:	1
	2012 Spanish GP
Poles:	1
Fastest laps:	0
Points:	47
Honours:	2010 GP2 CHAMPION,
	2004 ITALIAN FORMULA RENAULT
	CHAMPION, 2003 ITALIAN FORMULA
	RENAULT WINTER CHAMPION

SERVING HIS APPRENTICESHIP

Pastor deserved a prize for perseverance when he made it to Formula One back in 2011, as he'd spent the previous eight years living far from home as he attempted to scale the single-seater ladder to get there. Fortunately, he had an appreciable budget from Venezuela. Without it, his erratic form would have seen him sidelined before he reached it. Back in 2003, when he based himself in Italy in 2003 to try Formula Renault, it was already plain that he was quick – but, as he advanced to more powerful categories, he showed that he was also prone to accidents. Two years in Formula Renault were followed by two years in the Renault World Series, where he ranked third in 2006. Then came a four-year stint in F1's antechamber, GP2. He won races in each of the first three years, but only came good in 2010 when he won six of the 20 races for Rapax to beat Sergio Perez to the title. Williams took him on for 2011, with his healthy budget a definite factor, and he has had one stand-out result, victory in Spain in 2012.

McLAREN

Things can only improve for McLaren after a grim season in 2013 when former grand prix winner Jenson Button couldn't even score a podium finish. The team's big hope is that its revised design team proves best at interpreting the new rules.

Jenson Button's disappointment at the team's form in 2013 might be assuaged by the fact that it started developing its 2014 car early.

McLaren's excellence has been a factor for so long that it seems wrong to look ahead to a grand prix and not have a McLaren in the mix for victory. Yet this was the case throughout 2013, and it seemed very strange indeed to see its drivers scrapping for the minor points placings, and sometimes even further back, especially as it had closed its 2012 campaign with Jenson Button winning the Brazilian GP.

Certainly, matters weren't helped by technical director Paddy Lowe leaving during last season to go to Mercedes AMG Petronas just when he could have been focused on helping to sort the problem that stemmed from what was described as "different departments having worked at cross purposes". Tim Goss has stepped up to fill the role and Matt Morris was signed from Sauber to become director of engineering.

Late last year team principal Martin Whitmarsh signed aerodynamicist Peter Prodromou from Red Bull. Had he not, it would have been like the manager of a top football team failing to make any summer signings and thus giving his team the image of being less than desirable. Yes, teams' design departments are now so huge that the "names" at the top are only the tip of the iceberg, but their very presence is what gives the management the ability to convince sponsors and drivers alike to commit.

KEY MOMENTS AND KEY PEOPLE

TIM GOSS

Trained as a specialist in turbocharged engines, Tim worked for Cosworth from 1986 until he joined McLaren in 1990. His first responsibility was engine installation, but he became more hands-on when made Mika Hakkinen's assistant race engineer, and was then put in charge of the test team. Appointed chief engineer in 2005, Tim had responsibility for the design of the MP4-21, then the MP4-23 two years later as McLaren adopted a one year on, one year off approach. On Paddy Lowe's departure last year, he was made technical director.

GOLDEN YEAR: 1988

McLaren's duo from 1988 were stellar: Alain Prost and Ayrton Senna. Armed with the lowline, Honda-powered MP4/4, they took control from the first race and left their rivals way behind. The only battle was between the two of them, with Senna just coming out ahead for his first world title. Had he not clipped a backmarker in the Italian GP, they would have won all 16 rounds.

2013 DRIVERS & RESULTS

Driver	Nationality	Races	Wins	Pts	Pos
Jenson Button	British	19	0	73	9th
Sergio Perez	Mexican	19	0	49	11th

It seems crazy to even link McLaren to this sort of situation, especially bearing in mind its extraordinary levels of professionalism and its considerable success over the decades, but last year was not a good one for the team. Indeed, there were more than a few races in which its cars weren't competitive enough to offer the drivers a shot at scoring points, as their comparative speed against the other teams dropped back from fastest in 2012 to only sixth fastest last year, losing 1.313s per lap on average. Fortunately, development parts introduced after the British GP improved matters, and the points started to flow, albeit at a rate with which McLaren would have been disappointed in previous years.

In among this loss of form, Sergio Perez was felt not to have met the team's expectations of him when it signed the Mexican from Sauber. There were days when he could match Button in qualifying, and late in the year he outraced him, but the team had hoped for more from him. This is why it considered Nico Hulkenberg as a replacement before eliminating him from the reckoning for being too tall and too heavy before opting for rookie Kevin Magnussen.

It's excusable for many of the staff to be heading into 2014 with one eye on the future, as McLaren will have a new engine partner next year when it will end its deal with Mercedes-Benz and restart its partnership with Honda after a 22-year break. If this Anglo-Japanese partnership works as well as before – it won the constructors' title each year from 1988 to 1991 – then the other teams will have plenty to fear. Even though the team will never have another Ayrton Senna – he won three of the drivers' titles in this spell and Alain Prost won the other – there's considerable anticipation about how Honda might help the team rediscover a cutting edge that was so needed last year.

> "F1 is a relentlessly demanding sport and this season's new regulations have presented the teams with a daunting array of technical challenges – not only powertrains, but aerodynamics too."
> **Martin Whitmarsh**

Martin Whitmarsh in a rare light-hearted moment in 2013. There should be more smiles in 2014.

JENSON BUTTON

Last year was an annus horribilis for Jenson, by far his worst in Formula One since his Honda Racing days, as he had to make do with a car that was far from being the pick of the pack. Now he really needs McLaren to get back on song.

Jenson's Formula One career has been very much one of ups and downs, such as his time with BAR and Honda Racing – before it morphed into Brawn GP for 2009 and he responded by winning the drivers' title. On joining McLaren in 2010, he must have thought that those days were over, that this long-established team was stable enough to ensure that he would always be in with a shout of victory, if not the title.

And so it proved, as he ranked fifth, second and fifth again in his first three years. Then came last year, and the wins that he'd gathered in each of those previous years dried up. Indeed, the best he could manage was ninth place overall in the championship, with a best finish of fourth place at the season-closing Brazilian GP. His mood plummeted once it became clear that the team had no quick-fix solution and he had to make do with running around outside the top six.

If McLaren can do its sums right and build a competitive car, Jenson will surely shine again and reap the rewards for supporting the team through its tough time. Then, hopefully, the smile and charm

Jenson lost his smile in 2013 but will laugh again if McLaren gets its car right in 2014.

will return. If not, then he will find his 15th season in racing's top formula a drag of even greater proportions than last year's, the extra rounds a curse rather than a blessing.

Now one of the sport's elder statesmen, Jenson is aware that the clock is ticking but a better campaign this year will surely keep him with the team for 2015, when McLaren welcomes on board Honda once more in its quest to return to the McLaren-Honda glory days of the late 1980s and early 1990s.

TRACK NOTES

Nationality:	BRITISH
Born:	19 JANUARY 1980, FROME, ENGLAND
Website:	www.jensonbutton.com
Teams:	WILLIAMS 2000, BENETTON/RENAULT 2001-02, BAR/HONDA 2003-08, BRAWN 2009, McLAREN 2010-14

CAREER RECORD

First Grand Prix:	2000 AUSTRALIAN GP
Grand Prix starts:	248
Grand Prix wins:	15
	2006 Hungarian GP, 2009 Australian GP, Malaysian GP, Bahrain GP, Spanish GP, Monaco GP, Turkish GP, 2010 Australian GP, Chinese GP, 2011 Canadian GP, Hungarian GP, Japanese GP, 2012 Australian GP, Belgian GP, Brazilian GP
Poles:	8
Fastest laps:	8
Points:	1072
Honours:	2009 FORMULA ONE WORLD CHAMPION, 1999 MACAU FORMULA THREE RUNNER-UP, 1998 FORMULA FORD FESTIVAL WINNER, BRITISH FORMULA FORD CHAMPION & McLAREN AUTOSPORT BRDC YOUNG DRIVER, 1997 EUROPEAN SUPER A KART CHAMPION, 1991 BRITISH CADET KART CHAMPION

COMING BACK FOR MORE

Jenson was always likely to race, as his father competed in rallycross in the 1970s and so racing was in his bloodline. So, as soon as he was eight, Jenson started racing karts and by 11 he was British Cadet Kart Champion. By 17, he had been crowned as European champion. His first year of car racing, in Formula Ford 1600, landed Jenson the British title, the Formula Festival trophy and, vitally, the McLaren Autosport BRDC Young Driver of the Year award. This raised his profile, and he boosted it further by shining in F3. Then, thanks to his management team, he landed a Ligier F1 test and did so well that Williams signed him for 2000. Benetton and Renault weren't so competitive when he raced with them, so he moved to BAR in 2003 and he ranked third in 2004. However, it took until 2006, by which time the team was called Honda, for Jenson to take his first win. When the team was reinvented as Brawn in 2009, it produced the best car to help Jenson become World Champion. He joined McLaren in 2010.

KEVIN MAGNUSSEN

Groomed for stardom by McLaren, Kevin was offered a plum drive for 2014 after outpacing Sergio Perez on the simulator. There will be no training year with a tail-end team, instead a very real chance to exceed his father's one-race stay at McLaren.

Of all the signings for 2014, Kevin's has the potential to be a great one. His is the signing that is a breath of fresh air. This isn't just because he's a new face, like Russians Sergei Sirotkin or Daniil Kvyat, but also because he has proved his credentials to a far greater extent and looks to have the tools to deliver what's expected of him. This is a real case of signing a driver for his talent rather than his potential or, sadly, for the budget that he can bring.

Kevin has been on McLaren's books since 2012, augmenting test runs with plenty of time on its simulator and attending grands prix to learn how an F1 driver is expected to glean the most from a grand prix meeting.

There is also a family connection with the team as his father Jan raced for McLaren, just the once, in 1995. This was at the Pacific GP at the Aida circuit, when he was promoted from his test driving role to stand in for Mika Hakkinen when the Finn had appendicitis. Jan would later race for Stewart GP.

What was notable last year was how Kevin added consistency and common sense to his undoubted speed behind

Kevin is highly rated by McLaren and knows that he has been given a fabulous chance.

the wheel, with his team boss at DAMS, Jean-Paul Driot, commenting "Kevin is very good mentally and he knows how to manage everything and so won't be distracted by all that F1 brings."

Thanks to the wholesale change to F1's

technical regulations, it's unlikely that McLaren will produce a car as far from the pace as its 2013 challenger, so Kevin will undoubtedly find himself in a better position as the team's number-two driver than Sergio Perez did last year.

It's also clear that the team decided that Kevin is easily good enough for it not to be considered a risk to pick him in place of Perez, a driver with three years of F1 experience.

The opportunity to come into F1 with a top team is extremely rare and this long-time frontrunning outfit proved in 2007, when it elevated Lewis Hamilton to a race seat, that it's more than happy to help its young guns to shine.

TRACK NOTES

Nationality:	DANISH
Born:	5 OCTOBER 1992, ROSKILDE, DENMARK
Website:	www.kevinmagnussen.com
Teams:	McLAREN 2014

CAREER RECORD

First Grand Prix:	2014 AUSTRALIAN GP
Grand Prix starts:	0
Grand Prix wins:	0
Poles:	0
Fastest laps:	0
Points:	0
Honours:	2013 FORMULA RENAULT 3.5 CHAMPION, 2011 BRITISH FORMULA THREE RUNNER-UP, 2009 FORMULA RENAULT NORTHERN EUROPE RUNNER-UP, 2008 DANISH FORMULA FORD CHAMPION

FOLLOWING AFTER HIS FATHER

Racing is coursing through Kevin's veins since his father Jan was a racer when Kevin was born and continues to race today, many years after his shot at Formula One ended in disappointment after he was dropped by Stewart GP midway through 1998. Kevin was put on a racing kart as soon as he was old enough, and the speed he developed in this served him well when he graduated to car racing in 2008 at the age of 15 and won his national Formula Ford title. In 2009, Kevin advanced to Formula Renault and finished as runner-up to Antonio Felix da Costa in the lesser Northern European series before stepping up to Formula Three in 2010. Racing in Germany, he was top rookie before moving on to race for Carlin in the British series in 2011. After ranking second in that, Kevin won the Formula Renault 3.5 series at the second attempt in 2013 and did so in a manner that thoroughly impressed McLaren as he left pre-season favourite da Costa third.

Jenson Button could only go as fast as his McLaren would allow him in 2013, but sixth in Belgium showed that the team's form was improving.

SAHARA FORCE INDIA

There were times last year when Force India was in the thick of things. However, the team cannot bank on McLaren (and even Ferrari) dropping points again, so expect more of a struggle as the order is re-established in 2014.

Paul di Resta and Adrian Sutil endured an up and down season in 2013, but finance rather than form was a deciding factor in who drove in 2014.

Team owner Vijay Mallya had every reason to smile last year. His companies might have been financially beleaguered and his airline grounded, but his cars were snapping at the heels of those from teams with a far more established reputation. Better than that, they were ahead of the McLarens on points for much of the year, their raw pace marginally superior to the similarly Mercedes-powered cars from Woking.

A speed comparison made two-thirds of the way through the 2013 season showed that the Force Indias had actually dropped marginally further from the ultimate pace relative to their proximity to pace-setters McLaren in 2012. Mercedes had taken over in 2013 and were ranked top due to their prowess in qualifying. However, the Force Indias had advanced by three positions to be ranked fifth fastest, behind Mercedes, Red Bull, Ferrari and Lotus, but ahead of McLaren, Toro Rosso, Sauber, Williams, Caterham and Marussia.

The team's point-gathering through Adrian Sutil and Paul di Resta started in a hugely encouraging way with seventh and eighth places at the opening round in Melbourne, and by early autumn Force India was usually the sixth fastest team, thus forcing its drivers to snap around just outside the points, having ranked fifth

KEY MOMENTS AND KEY PEOPLE

VIJAY MALLYA
This Indian industrialist's involvement with motor racing dates back to long before he bought the controlling stake in the team in 2008 and changed its name from Spyker to Force India. He had raced powerful single-seaters in the non-championship Indian GP in the late 1980s. Later, he began to put the name of his Kingfisher beer on the side of cars, like the Benetton F1 cars, from 1996, and his involvement has grown from there. Away from the tracks, Vijay's Kingfisher airline was stopped from flying in 2012.

GOLDEN YEAR: 1999
Back in 1999, the team was still Jordan, racing in yellow and black and anxious to build on its first win, scored at Spa-Francorchamps the year before by Damon Hill when he led home team-mate Ralf Schumacher. As it turned out, Hill was eclipsed by new team-mate Heinz-Harald Frentzen, who not only won at Magny-Cours but did so again at Monza to help the team rank a career best third overall at the end of the year, albeit some way behind Ferrari and McLaren.

2013 DRIVERS & RESULTS

Driver	Nationality	Races	Wins	Pts	Pos
Paul di Resta	British	19	0	48	12th
Adrian Sutil	German	19	0	29	13th

FOR THE RECORD

Country of origin:	England
Team base:	Silverstone, England
Telephone:	(44) 01327 850800
Website:	www.forceindiaf1.com
Active in Formula One:	As Jordan 1991-2004, Midland 2005-06, Spyker 2007
Grands Prix contested:	397
Wins:	4
Pole positions:	3
Fastest laps:	4

THE TEAM

Team principal & managing director:	Vijay Mallya
Chairman:	Subrata Roy Sahara
Deputy team principal:	Robert Fernley
Chief operating officer:	Otmar Szafnauer
Technical director:	Andrew Green
Production director:	Bob Halliwell
Chief designers:	Akio Haga & Ian Hall
Aerodynamics director:	Simon Phillips
Sporting director:	Andy Stevenson
Chief engineer:	Jakob Andreasen
Test driver:	James Calado
Chassis:	Force India VJM07
Engine:	Mercedes V6
Tyres:	Pirelli

overall through much of the summer until McLaren finally moved ahead at the Belgian GP, the 11th of the season's 19 rounds. This was shortly after Pirelli had reverted to offering 2012-specification tyres, which Force India's VJM06s really didn't like. Indeed, their form took a dive. Perhaps because of having to try too hard to make up for this, di Resta then had a run of retirements caused by collisions and crashes, while Sutil was restricted to occasional ninth- and 10th-place finishes. By this stage, di Resta's fourth place at Sakhir and Sutil's fifth at Monaco seemed a distant memory as the drivers started to worry that they might not be kept on for 2014.

Despite the early-season progress made under technical director Andrew Green's guidance before Force India opted to swing its attention towards its 2014 design, the team continues to have hanging over it the spectre of an insufficient budget. Naturally, this not only affected whom the team could afford to bring in to bolster its design team, but its driver selection too, opening up a way in for a driver with a large budget. Di Resta knew that he had a contract for 2014, while Sutil didn't. At some point, former Force India racer Nico Hulkenberg was linked with a return to the team after his one-year sojourn with Sauber. Then, when it became clear that Williams and Pastor Maldonado were parting company and that he had the PDVSA money to bring with him, he moved into the mix, as did Sergio Perez with his Telmex backing after he was dropped by McLaren.

Mallya and deputy team principal Robert Fernley plumped for Nico Hulkenberg and Sergio Perez as its drivers for 2014 and they will all be hoping that several of the top teams trip up to the extent that they did in 2013. There is always scope for a team to find a technical advantage when there is a major change to Formula One's technical rulebook, but it tends to be the better-financed teams that find it, so perhaps Force India ought to expect to drop a position or two in this year's World Championship campaign.

"We have finished in the top six twice in the past three seasons, consolidating our reputation as being the best non-manufacturer team. It's a real credit to everyone at Force India."
Robert Fernley

Andrew Green had to guide the team back to form after last year's mid-season tyre change.

NICO HULKENBERG

Nico looked to have made a backwards step when he moved from Force India to Sauber in 2013, but then came good as the car improved. His expected move to Lotus fell through due to lack of funds, so he returns to Force India for 2014.

When Nico was finally confirmed as a Force India driver for 2014, he must have heaved a huge sigh of relief, as it seemed as though a new twist might scupper his F1 career just as he had demonstrated that he was the best of the drivers outside the top oufits.

One of the problems was his size. Nico is comparatively tall and heavy and this came into play when the teams discovered that the new turbo engines and energy retrieval systems were likely to weigh more than expected. So meeting the minimum weight (measured as the weight of the car plus the driver) was going to be a problem - overweight cars are at a performance disadvantage. Thus, to get close to their "fighting weight", teams were seeking lighter drivers than Nico. Also, being tall was seen as a problem for the snug cockpits the teams wanted to design.

But the main reason that his predicted move to Lotus failed to materialize was the team's continued financial concerns. With Pastor Maldonado and his PDVSA sponsorship on the move from Williams,

Nico provided some fireworks in 2013 and is hoping to provide some more this year.

it became clear that Nico, with no such backing, could not offer Lotus the cash that Maldonado could bring. So Nico returned to Force India, a team he knows very well.

The first half of 2013 didn't yield too many points for Nico as Sauber became less competitive. In fact, he felt that he'd made a duff move from Force India. Yet, the F1 paddock could see his potential and Nico was sought by several of the top teams. His run to fifth at Monza was impressive, but he topped this by finishing fourth in Korea after resisting intense pressure from Mercedes' Lewis Hamilton. Fernando Alonso, who closed in on the pair, described Nico's driving as "superb". High praise indeed.

TRACK NOTES

Nationality:	GERMAN
Born:	19 AUGUST 1987, EMMERICH, GERMANY
Website:	www.nicohulkenberg.net/en
Teams:	WILLIAMS 2010, FORCE INDIA 2012, SAUBER 2013, FORCE INDIA 2014

CAREER RECORD	
First Grand Prix:	2010 BAHRAIN GP
Grand Prix starts:	58
Grand Prix wins:	0
	(best result: 4th, 2012 Belgian GP, 2013 Korean GP)
Poles:	1
Fastest laps:	1
Points:	136
Honours:	2009 GP2 CHAMPION, 2008 EUROPEAN FORMULA THREE CHAMPION, 2007 FORMULA THREEE MASTERS WINNER, 2006/07 A1GP CHAMPION, 2005 GERMAN FORMULA BMW CHAMPION, 2003 GERMAN KART CHAMPION, 2002 GERMAN JUNIOR KART CHAMPION

TICKING ALL THE BOXES

Nico is a driver who lets his driving do the talking and who has made his way to Formula One on talent alone. After winning junior and senior German karting titles, he burst onto the country's car racing scene in 2005 and pipped the more experienced Sebastien Buemi to the Formula BMW crown. Driving a Ligier rather than the dominant Dallara hampered his first year of Formula Three, but he showed enough speed to be selected to race for Germany's A1GP team and was the stand-out driver in this international winter series for more powerful cars. Nico then carried on this form into the European F3 season, ranking third behind Romain Grosjean and Buemi. He then put this right by changing to the ART Grand Prix team and dominating the series in 2008. Stepping up to GP2 in 2009, Nico was a rare rookie champion. Williams gave him his F1 break in 2010, and he marked his year by taking pole in Brazil. Out of a drive in 2011, he bounced back in 2012 with Force India, leading in Brazil.

SERGIO PEREZ

Sergio would have hoped that McLaren was going to retain its usual front-running form in 2013. Alas, he picked the worst year possible to join the team, and his own lack of form through most of the season cost him his drive, forcing him to move on.

For 2014, Sergio Perez, aka "Checo", will be racing for Force India. McLaren's team principal Martin Whitmarsh was left remorseful after dropping the young Mexican to make way for the arrival of Danish rookie Kevin Magnussen, just as his form came good in the late-season races. Whitmarsh then pushed to try and find him a ride with another team.

Still, careers can have setbacks, and how a driver bounces back from disappointment can really demonstrate their character. Checo's setback may just give him the impetus he requires to raise his game to the next level.

Early last year, as he was trying to make his mark at McLaren with a car that was clearly less than competitive, the pressure to perform became clear when he had a disagreement with Jenson Button while scrapping over fifth place during the Bahrain GP at Sakhir, swapping positions and even rubbing wheels. His team-mate asked the team to tell Checo to "calm down", but the team declined to do so and then Button dropped back, after requiring an extra pitstop for fresh tyres, ending up in 10th place to Checo's sixth.

Sergio came on strong in 2013's closing races, but McLaren had decided to drop him.

It turns out that the team had chivvied Checo before the race to press harder, so they were hardly in a position to criticize him for doing just that.

However, his form then dropped away in the races as both he and, in fairness, Button too found their cars a handful. His qualifying pace was actually the equal of his team-mate's, but Checo's ability to preserve his tyres through the course of a grand prix was not. He did acknowledge, though, that he had learned an awful lot in adversity and will be the stronger for it.

For 2014, Checo has a new challenge and it will be intriguing to watch and see whether he can look like the young charger of 2012, when he shone for Sauber and pushed Fernando Alonso's Ferrari so hard for victory in a wet/dry Malaysian GP.

With the return of the Mexican GP expected for 2015, for the first time since 1992, the pressure is on for Checo to work himself back into a top drive.

TRACK NOTES

Nationality:	MEXICAN
Born:	26 JANUARY 1990, GUADALAJARA, MEXICO
Website:	www.sergioperez.mx
Teams:	SAUBER 2011-12, McLAREN 2013, FORCE INDIA 2014

CAREER RECORD

First Grand Prix:	2011 BAHRAIN GP
Grand Prix starts:	56
Grand Prix wins:	0
(best result: second, 2012 Malaysian GP)	
Poles:	0
Fastest laps:	2
Points:	129

Honours: 2010 GP2 RUNNER-UP, 2007 BRITISH FORMULA THREE NATIONAL CLASS CHAMPION

GETTING A HEAD START

Being permitted by his national sporting association to graduate to car racing at just 14 years of age gave Checo a head start over European rivals. This is the age at which he left Mexico for the USA to race in the Barber Dodge formula. He headed to Germany the following year, 2005, and raced in its Formula BMW series. He ranked sixth against his older rivals in 2006 and then progressed to Formula Three. Competing in the National class in the British series, he won that title, then stepped up to the main class in 2008 and ranked fourth as Jaime Alguersuari took the honours. Checo's first taste of power came in the GP2 Asia series later that year. Contesting the main GP2 series in 2009, he had a disappointing year. It was a different story in 2010, and he was runner-up to Pastor Maldonado. Then he was picked by Sauber for their 2011 F1 line-up, helped by backing from Mexico. In 2012, he came close to beating Ferrari's Fernando Alonso at Sepang and this form took him to McLaren.

SAUBER

The Mexican backing has gone for this team that has been living close to the edge, but Russian money has arrived in its place and people are watching to see whether this will be enough to help the Swiss team regain momentum.

Esteban Gutierrez came on strong through 2013 as the car came good and will be looking to build on that experience in 2014.

To see Nico Hulkenberg holding off a pack of cars containing Lewis Hamilton's Mercedes, Fernando Alonso's Ferrari and Jenson Button's McLaren for lap after lap to claim fourth place in last year's Korean GP was heart-warming. This wasn't only because it was another opportunity for the top teams' principals to see how good he was; it also meant that this team that had teetered close to the financial brink last year was able to collect a good helping of points – which are worth a lot when the prize money is divided up. This result moved the Swiss team ahead of Toro Rosso, so adding millions to the pot.

It seems a long time ago now that this team raced as BMW Sauber, as it did from 2006 to 2010, when there was money for in-season development. Last year's plain-looking car, with more space available on its flanks for sponsors than is healthy, was a sign that the team was struggling financially. There's no doubt that the lack of money available since has made it hard for the team to make progress, hard even to keep its design staff, but the arrival of backing from Russia could be the start of a new chapter.

The new money comes from a triumvirate of Russian companies looking to promote the country's technology businesses and also its global image. Many reckon that they were encouraged to become involved by President Putin, especially as the Russian GP at Sochi

KEY MOMENTS AND KEY PEOPLE

MONISHA KALTENBORN
Formula One's first female team chief, Monisha is an Austrian of Indian extraction who took a law degree in Vienna then a masters' degree at the London School of Economics. She came into contact with F1 while working for the Fritz Kaiser Group in 1999 when it bought a share of Sauber. A member of the team's management since 2001, she became CEO in 2010, and was given a third share of the team by Peter Sauber in 2012, becoming team principal when Peter stepped back later that year.

GOLDEN YEAR: 2008
Sauber, or BMW Sauber as it was then, was a team on the up in 2008. It had a great driver pairing in consistent Nick Heidfeld and flying hotshot Robert Kubica. The German had finished second in the first race in Australia, something the Pole matched at the next race, in Malaysia, and which he followed with third place in Bahrain. After another second place for Kubica, in Monaco, the team hit gold in Canada when Kubica headed a Sauber one-two. They ranked third.

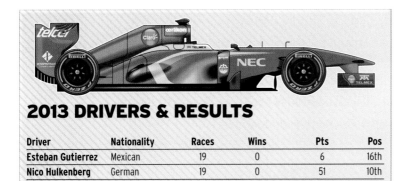

2013 DRIVERS & RESULTS

Driver	Nationality	Races	Wins	Pts	Pos
Esteban Gutierrez	Mexican	19	0	6	16th
Nico Hulkenberg	German	19	0	51	10th

FOR THE RECORD

Country of origin:	Switzerland
Team base:	Hinwil, Switzerland
Telephone:	(41) 44 937 9000
Website:	www.sauberf1team.com
Active in Formula One:	From 1993
	(as BMW Sauber 2006-10)
Grands Prix contested:	364
Wins:	1
Pole positions:	1
Fastest laps:	5

is one of his projects. There is another factor in their involvement, too, as young racer Sergey Sirotkin's father is head of the first of these bodies, which is why he was tipped for a race seat for 2014 until it became clear that he hadn't enough experience to be granted the required FIA superlicence.

There is also an interesting consideration regarding the involvement of the State Fund for the Development of the North-Western Russian Federation: it suggests that Russia might at some stage move its grand prix away from Sochi and relocate it in St Petersburg, where this fund is based.

Team principal Monisha Kaltenborn says that the deal is more than just a financial one, as it also includes the establishment of a joint development centre that will be "not just about technology transfer, but about technology creation", with the ambition to spread jointly developed technology way beyond the motor sport industry. Other elements of the deal are the aims of establishing F1 better in Russia through the team's performance and helping to develop up-and-coming Russian racing talent.

Last year, the team had a mid-season change of form, corresponding not just with some minor aerodynamic tweaks, but also with the arrival of the 2012-style control tyre that clearly suited the C32. Both Nico and

Esteban made progress thereafter, as the German showed at Monza, qualifying third and then racing to fifth, then again in Korea when he finished a fabulous fourth.

For 2014, Sauber will have to do without Hulkenberg's talents. Adrian Sutil will lead the team and, Sauber hopes he'll share his experience with second season racer Gutierrez, with both helping to bring teenaged reserve Sergey Sirotkin along.

There is a change on the technical side, with chief designer Matt Morris heading to McLaren a year after joining from Williams, leaving head of aerodynamics Willem Toet in charge of the shaping of this year's C33.

THE TEAM

Team principal:	Monisha Kaltenborn
Operations director:	Axel Kruse
Chief designer:	Eric Gandelin
Head of aerodynamics:	Willem Toet
Head of car performance:	Ben Waterhouse
Head of track engineering:	Tom McCullough
Senior strategist:	Giampaolo Dall'ara
Team manager:	Beat Zehnder
Test driver:	TBA
Chassis:	Sauber C33
Engine:	Ferrari V6
Tyres:	Pirelli

"If you look at the history of our team, we have often had two young and not very experienced drivers and yet we often did some of our best seasons with them."

Monisha Kaltenborn

Willem Toet has been responsible for the C33 following Matt Morris's departure to McLaren.

ADRIAN SUTIL

Last year was a frustrating one for Adrian as his Force India team lost form midway through the season. This year, after an unusually busy period on the driver merry-go-round, he has ended up with Sauber and has a point to prove.

The winter of 2013-14 was an exceptional one for the Formula One driver market as an unusually high number of team changes were effected, driven as ever by moves among the top teams. The fall-out from this, as well as from a general shortage of budget for teams in the midfield and below, was more movement of drivers than F1 is accustomed to. As one of the drivers with a degree of backing, Adrian Sutil was in a position to survive in this game of musical chairs, unlike his 2013 Force India team-mate Paul di Resta, who lost his drive.

So, thanks to his backing from the Medion computer company, he has kept his place on the grid, albeit moving from Force India to fellow midfielders Sauber in order to do so.

Adrian's 2013 season offered promise after a year without a drive following an assault charge levelled at him, and he soon showed that he hadn't lost any pace during his time on the sidelines when he led the opening round in Australia, adopting a different race strategy to his rivals and then finishing in seventh place. After some ill fortune cost him strong

Adrian made a strong return to racing in 2013 but had to move teams for 2014.

finishes in China, Bahrain and Spain, Adrian did better still in the sixth round by finishing fifth at Monaco.

However, his team lost form after those early races, especially when the 2012 tyre compounds were reintroduced midway through the year. Records will show that team-mate di Resta scored more points than he did across the season's 19 grands prix – 48 to 29 – and Adrian certainly was far from complimentary about the car they drove.

At season's end, Sauber appeared to have a faster car than Force India did, so perhaps he will be taking a small step forward, unless the Sauber was flattered in a big way by the driving of Nico Hulkenberg.

Yet, with the all-encompassing new rules and both teams suffering from uncertain financial situations, nothing can be taken for granted.

40

TRACK NOTES

Nationality: GERMAN
Born: 11 JANUARY 1983, STARNBERG, GERMANY
Website: www.adrian-sutil.de
Teams: SPYKER/FORCE INDIA 2007-11 & 2013, SAUBER 2014

CAREER RECORD

First Grand Prix:	2007 AUSTRALIAN GP
Grand Prix starts:	109
Grand Prix wins:	0
	(best result: 4th, 2009 Italian GP)
Poles:	0
Fastest laps:	1
Points:	124

Honours: 2006 JAPANESE FORMULA THREE CHAMPION, 2005 EUROPEAN FORMULA THREE RUNNER-UP, 2002 SWISS FORMULA FORD CHAMPION

ADRIAN'S STOP-START CAREER

A first run in a kart can be a pivotal moment in many a young racer's life. Adrian was a talented musician, following in his father's footsteps, but then came that run in a kart. After four years of kart racing, Adrian won the Swiss Formula Ford Championship. In 2003, he moved to the German Formula BMW ADAC series and ranked sixth. Stepping up to Formula Three, Adrian showed flashes of speed in 2004, then started winning in 2005 when he ended the year as runner-up to his team-mate Lewis Hamilton. After gaining a taste of power in A1GP, he moved to Japan and won their F3 title. A promising test with the Spyker F1 team landed him his F1 break for 2007 and he stayed on for the next four years as it changed into Force India, scoring fourth place at Monza in 2009. There was a hiatus after he was accused of assaulting a Lotus F1 team shareholder in 2011, and this kept him out of racing until he returned in 2013.

ESTEBAN GUTIERREZ

Having Nico Hulkenberg as a team-mate will make any driver look slow in comparison, but Esteban made a marked improvement through his rookie season and is now back to show that he can build on that experience.

There's no Mexican GP on the 2014 World Championship calendar after it was proposed then dropped before last year was out. However, there will almost certainly be one in 2015 once the Autodromo Hermanos Rodriguez in the outskirts of Mexico City has been brought up to contemporary standards, and this is one of the reasons why Esteban has been able to stay for a second year with Sauber despite being outscored 51 points to six by team-mate Nico Hulkenberg last year.

Formula One has regained its profile in Mexico decades after it was replaced in the fans' affections by Indycar racing. Having a grand prix for the home fans will inevitably boost that new-found passion further, but that requires at least one Mexican driver to be on the starting grid. To this end, billionaire Carlos Slim is bankrolling the careers of both Esteban and Sergio Perez, which explains why Esteban is able to continue in F1 while more established drivers like Paul di Resta have lost their places.

It might be said that Esteban's form in last year's early-season races disappointed,

Esteban took a while to get going last year but could blossom on his return in 2014.

as his best finish was 11th in Spain, but the Swiss team's drivers were both finding it hard to be competitive with the C32, and Esteban seemed to be struggling to learn how to offer the technical feedback that a team requires.

However, Esteban persevered and began to get closer to Hulkenberg's pace in qualifying. Then, late in the season, he got closer to the highly respected German in the races too, and did well to score his first ever world championship points with seventh place at the Japanese GP at Suzuka.

There was an unsettling atmosphere last autumn when Russian investment in Sauber looked as though it might cost Esteban his drive for 2014, but Sergey Sirotkin not being awarded the superlicence he needs to race in F1 left the door open for Esteban to have another crack at the big time, and it will be intriguing to see if he can continue the progress he made last year.

TRACK NOTES

Nationality:	MEXICAN
Born:	5 AUGUST 1991, MONTERREY, MEXICO
Website:	www.estebanracing.com
Teams:	SAUBER 2013-14

CAREER RECORD	
First Grand Prix:	2013 AUSTRALIAN GP
Grand Prix starts:	19
Grand Prix wins:	0
	(best result: 7th, 2013 Japanese GP)
Poles:	0
Fastest laps:	0
Points:	6
Honours:	2010 GP3 CHAMPION, 2008 EUROPEAN FORMULA BMW CHAMPION, 2007 UNITED STATES FORMULA BMW RUNNER-UP, 2005 MEXICAN ROTAX MAX KART CHAMPION

READY FOR MEXICO'S F1 REVIVAL

With talk of Mexico eventually returning to the World Championship, it's fortunate timing for both Esteban and compatriot Sergio Perez that the level of interest from their home country has never been higher. Neither could have predicted that as they set out on their racing careers. Indeed, Esteban wasn't even a year old when Mexico last hosted a grand prix. After shining on the Mexican karting scene, Esteban advanced to cars by contesting the United States Formula BMW Championship and was runner-up in that at the age of 16. A move to Europe followed in 2008 and he immediately won the European Formula BMW title. In 2009, he not only raced in Formula Three but had an F1 test with Sauber, starting a relationship that would bear fruit. A move to the new GP3 series in 2010 paid off as he won the championship. Then came GP2 and he ranked third in that at his second attempt, but sponsorship of Sauber from Mexican sources put him in line for the team's second race seat.

SCUDERIA TORO ROSSO

This midfield team is a great place for Red Bull to place up-and-coming drivers on its books to see whether they can develop to the level required for a step up to Red Bull Racing – by showing they have the potential to become World Champion.

Jean-Eric Vergne is now Toro Rosso's undisputed team leader but he will be kept on his toes if Daniil Kvyat is as fast as people say he is.

For the first time since Sebastian Vettel stepped up at the end of the 2008 season, Scuderia Toro Rosso can head into a new season knowing that it has again served its primary purpose and fed another driver into Red Bull's lead team. Thus in 2014 all eyes will be on Daniel Ricciardo at Red Bull Racing to see how he shapes up alongside Vettel.

As for the Toro Rosso driver left behind, Jean-Eric Vergne, he will have to dust himself off and continue to push for promotion to the big time, not that it looks as though Vettel will be leaving a vacancy any time soon. He knows that the decision was a tough one, and that his results all but matched Ricciardo's last year, but the team will expect him to keep pushing hard and that new signing Daniil Kvyat gets up to speed as soon as possible after graduating from CP3 as champion as the new driver on the Red Bull junior scheme. Of course, Toro Rosso would be guaranteed more points in the year ahead if it simply employed one of the established F1 drivers from another team, but that's not why Toro Rosso exists. It's a training ground. Its effectiveness is also maximized if its cars can be competitive enough to get in the points, thus giving its pair of drivers the chance to spend the year battling with the sort of drivers that they will be expected to beat in the years ahead if ever promoted to Red Bull Racing.

KEY MOMENTS AND KEY PEOPLE

HELMUT MARKO
Dietrich Mateschitz's talent spotter certainly knows his stuff, having raced in Formula One before his career was cut short when a stone pierced his visor in the 1972 French GP, blinding him in one eye. While gaining his doctorate in law, Helmut shone in Formula Super Vee, then made a name for himself in sportscars before being given his F1 break by BRM in 1971. Later, when fellow Austrian Mateschitz decided to put money from his energy drink company into racing, he chose Helmut to advise him.

GOLDEN YEAR: 2008
After 21 years of struggle as Minardi, a cash injection from Red Bull in 2006 led to the team being renamed Scuderia Toro Rosso. The third year with the energy drink company's money behind it was a quantum leap as Sebastian Vettel built on the fourth place he'd scored in China in 2007, gathering points through 2008 before revealing the extent of his talent by being in total control at a rain-hit Monza. With Sebastien Bourdais's slim points tally, the team ranked sixth.

2013 DRIVERS & RESULTS

Driver	Nationality	Races	Wins	Pts	Pos
Daniel Ricciardo	Australian	19	0	20	14th
Jean-Eric Vergne	French	19	0	13	15th

FOR THE RECORD

Country of origin:	Italy
Team base:	Faenza, Italy
Telephone:	(39) 546 696111
Website:	www.scuderiatororosso.com
Active in Formula One:	As Minardi 1995-2005
Grands Prix contested:	488
Wins:	1
Pole positions:	0
Fastest laps:	0

THE TEAM

Team owner:	Dietrich Mateschitz
Team principal:	Franz Tost
Technical director:	James Key
Sporting director:	Steve Nielsen
Chief designer:	Luca Furbatto
Head of aerodynamics:	Brendan Gilhome
Head of vehicle performance:	Laurent Mekies
Test driver:	TBA
Chassis:	Toro Rosso STR9
Engine:	Ferrari V6
Tyres:	Pirelli

Last year, with Red Bull Racing proving so dominant at the front of the field, Mercedes having stepped up a level and Lotus too, with Ferrari treading water and McLaren going backwards, it was hard for Toro Rosso's drivers to score points. The team's best result was JEV's sixth place in Canada, while Ricciardo twice brought his car home seventh, at Shanghai and Monza. Along with Force India, Sauber and sometimes Williams, there will be races at which they can gather a few points and others where they can't, but the aim for 2014 is to make sure that there will be more times that they can.

Franz Tost remains as Toro Rosso's team principal, but the team's strongest card is seen as technical director James Key, who arrived from Sauber for 2013. This year's car will be the first on which he has been involved from the outset of the project, and it's obviously a vital year to be doing so because of the comprehensive compromises brought about by the changes in the rules. If Key can interpret the various new factors right, there's a chance that Vergne and his new team-mate will be able to gain ground on their midfield rivals. Should they do so, then this modest man will get more recognition for his great design than he would have if

he'd elected to join a larger team – as had been his earlier intention when he was linked with Lotus – and perhaps become a little lost in the management. If he can carry on the team's recent tradition of building a car that is light on its tyres, then expect the STR9s once again to race better than they qualify.

Insiders see Key as a man with a big future, some even suggesting that he might one day replace Red Bull's chief technical officer Adrian Newey at Red Bull Racing, and that tells you all you need to know about how he's rated.

"It's a frustration to lose Daniel Ricciardo to Red Bull Racing as you always want to hang on to your drivers if they're doing a good job for you, but it shows that the Red Bull process works."

James Key

Franz Tost will have to manage a change in personnel as he welcomes Russian Daniil Kvyat.

JEAN-ERIC VERGNE

The disappointment of losing out to team-mate Daniel Ricciardo in the chase for the cherished second Red Bull Racing seat will still grate with JEV, but it will also give him extra impetus to prove his worth in his third year with Scuderia Toro Rosso.

The difference between success and failure in motor racing can often be measured in fractions of a second, and this is how Jean-Eric must feel after losing out in the selection process to replace Mark Webber last year at Red Bull Racing. For that was the sort of difference between him and his Australian team-mate Daniel Ricciardo. Indeed, JEV raced every bit as well, sometimes being better at bringing home any points available. His sixth place in the Canadian GP was an example of that. In the final analysis, though, JEV will be painfully aware that rides like the one Ricciardo landed come around only very rarely, so it's not as though a blindingly good string of results through 2014 will earn him a similar opportunity.

Also, to which team would his long-time backers Red Bull move him in order to improve his chances of winning? Not to any of the other teams that rank between itself and Scuderia Toro Rosso, that much is for sure …

So, JEV may have to focus on working on his qualifying speed, his one perceived weakness, although seventh on the grid

Jean-Eric needs to deliver qualifying laps that match his clear racing abilities.

in Canada last year showed that he can produce a great lap. If he can do this on a regular basis, he will have more of a chance to display his undoubted race craft and thus make himself more attractive to

the other teams to whom he may have to look if he is to advance.

JEV knows that he can't stay at Toro Rosso indefinitely, as Red Bull has its next handful of young drivers to bring on, so this is, in many ways, a make or break year for this 23-year-old. He's seen as a quick learner, so he'll have to do just this in 2014 to keep his name in lights.

To be the top Frenchman in Formula One, he has to beat Romain Grosjean, while behind him he also has Jules Bianchi learning his craft with Marussia.

TRACK NOTES

Nationality:	FRENCH
Born:	25 APRIL 1990, PONTOISE, FRANCE
Website:	www.jeanericvergne.com
Teams:	TORO ROSSO 2012-14

CAREER RECORD	
First Grand Prix:	2012 AUSTRALIAN GP
Grand Prix starts:	39
Grand Prix wins:	0 (best result: 6th, 2013 Canadian GP)
Poles:	0
Fastest laps:	0
Points:	29
Honours:	2011 FORMULA RENAULT 3.5 RUNNER-UP, 2010 BRITISH FORMULA THREE CHAMPION, 2009 EUROPEAN FORMULA RENAULT RUNNER-UP & WESTERN EUROPE RUNNER-UP, 2008 FRENCH FORMULA RENAULT CHAMPION, 2007 FRENCH FORMULA CAMPUS CHAMPION, 2006 FRENCH KART RUNNER-UP, 2005 EUROPEAN ICA KART RUNNER-UP, 2001 FRENCH CADET KART CHAMPION

A DRIVER WITH A LOT OF TITLES

Having a father who raced karts meant that Jean-Eric was always likely to follow that route, and he first drove one at the age of four. It came as no surprise, then, when Jean-Eric won the French Cadet title at the age of 11 and went on to become runner-up in the European ICA series in 2005, then runner-up in the French championship in 2006. France's Formula Campus was his first car racing series, and Jean-Eric dominated that in 2007 before spending a couple of years in Formula Renault, finishing as runner-up to Albert Costa in the European series in 2009. In 2010 he became the first French driver to win the British Formula Three title and showed great promise in five outings in Formula Renault 3.5 later that year, winning one of these. He stayed on in this more powerful category in 2011 and just failed to overhaul Canada's Robert Wickens at the final round. Having had an F1 test with Scuderia Toro Rosso in 2010, he had another and earned himself a race seat for 2012, going on to outscore his team-mate Daniel Ricciardo.

DANIIL KVYAT

There was considerable interest last October when news broke that this talented young Russian had filled the second Toro Rosso seat ahead of more experienced drivers. He will have to prove in 2014 that he hasn't been promoted too soon.

Not 20 years old until after this year's fourth round, the Chinese GP in Shanghai, there can be no doubting that Daniil has got to F1 young.

It has happened before, of course. Take Sebastian Vettel who was also still in his teens when he hit F1, but the now four-time World Champion had had a more structured career progression. Vitally, Vettel had won more championships on the way up.

Yet, those who have watched Daniil's early career all say that he possesses incredible natural speed. Red Bull young driver project supremo Helmut Marko says that he will have had to spend the winter improving his fitness, but that the raw pace is there. The question is whether Daniil can gain experience fast enough alongside Jean-Eric Vergne at Scuderia Toro Rosso to harness that without making a string of mistakes in his early races in this most testing of arenas.

To his credit, Daniil's form improved markedly through 2013, as shown by his trio of pole positions for the European F3 round at the Red Bull Ring, which resulted in a trio of second-place finishes for

Daniil came on strong last year and is very much favoured by Red Bull's talent spotters.

eventual series runner-up Felix Rosenqvist. He would later win the opening race at Zandvoort from pole, but as he hadn't had a regular drive in this series with Carlin, he wasn't eligible for points.

In GP3, running with MW Arden,

Daniil grabbed late-season wins at Spa-Francorchamps and Monza to move into title contention behind Facu Regalia. Then, while he peaked for the final two races in Abu Dhabi, the Argentinian's season fell apart and he failed to score as Daniil added a win from pole in the first race to clinch the title.

So, F1 is a considerable step forward, but not insurmountable if he's good enough and has the mental strength to be able to focus on the driving in this high-pressure environment. His arrival at the top of the sport is of course timely indeed with Russia finally claiming a place on the World Championship calendar. By the time the circus gets to Sochi, hopefully he will have made himself at home.

TRACK NOTES

Nationality:	RUSSIAN
Born:	26 APRIL 1994, UFA, RUSSIA
Website:	www.daniilkvyat.com
Teams:	TORO ROSSO 2014

CAREER RECORD

First Grand Prix:	2014 AUSTRALIAN GP
Grand Prix starts:	0
Grand Prix wins:	0
Poles:	0
Fastest laps:	0
Points:	0
Honours:	2013 GP3 CHAMPION, 2012 EUROPEAN FORMULA RENAULT RUNNER-UP & FORMULA RENAULT ALPS CHAMPION, 2011 FORMULA RENAULT NORTHERN EUROPE RUNNER-UP, 2009 WSK KART RUNNER-UP

CRISS-CROSSING THE GLOBE

Perhaps it was down to wanting to escape the freezing winters of Bashkortostan, but Daniil has been happy to travel far to gain experience in as short a time as possible. This had him venturing to New Zealand for the Toyota Racing Series at the start of 2011, and he won once to rank an eventual fifth overall. This was his springboard into a first full season of Formula Renault after a couple of taster races at the end of his first year of car racing that had been spent in Formula BMW. He ranked third in the European series behind Robin Frijns and Carlos Sainz Jr and finished as runner-up to Sainz Jr in the lesser Northern European Countries series. In 2012, Daniil advanced to be runner-up in the European series, behind Stoffel Vandoorne, and landed the title in the lesser ALPS Formula Renault series, but knew his career was on the way as he became a member of the Red Bull Junior Team, easing his passage to Formula Three and GP3 for 2013.

Esteban Gutierrez struggled through the first half of his rookie F1 campaign with Sauber but showed real progress later in the year to score his first points.

WILLIAMS

Things are stirring at Williams, and the arrival of Mercedes engines combined with new technical director Pat Symonds may lead to stronger results, something that is needed after last year, when there was no hint of a repetition of its one win of 2012.

Last year's Williams FW35 was far from the most competitive car to come from Grove and both Pastor Maldonado and Valtteri Bottas struggled.

For a team that has always had incredible stability on its management side, there has been a lot happening at Williams in the past few years. Toto Wolff, not long the team's executive director, left last year to head to Mercedes to replace Nick Fry as the person in charge of the day-to-day running of the team. His departure left a vacancy at the top of the team that was filled from within as Sir Frank's daughter Claire stepped up to be in charge of the team on a day-to-day basis.

However, Wolff's move to Mercedes also led to Williams changing its engine supplier from Renault, with a multi-year contract signed with the German manufacturer. Whether this proves to be a successful move or not remains to be seen, as no one knows how any of these new V6 turbos will perform relative to each other. Although using the new turbo V6s built by Mercedes AMG High Performance Powertrains at Brixworth in England, the team will continue to manufacture its own transmission.

Of course, there was some sadness at the end of the team's relationship with former engine partner Renault, as the companies have enjoyed considerable success together over the decades, most recently when Pastor Maldonado won the 2012 Spanish GP, but Williams very much sees the move to Mercedes as a positive one. "Mercedes-Benz has been one of the sport's most successful

KEY MOMENTS AND KEY PEOPLE

SIR FRANK WILLIAMS

No F1 team is as closely associated with one man as Williams is with its founder. He turned his back on his racing career after reaching F3, and then ran cars for others. His first driver, Piers Courage, was killed in the 1970 Dutch GP, but Frank kept on. The turning point came in linking up with engineer Patrick Head in the late 1970s. Alan Jones won them their first title in 1980, followed by Keke Rosberg, Nigel Mansell, Alain Prost, Damon Hill and Jacques Villeneuve, who won Williams' most recent title, in 1997.

GOLDEN YEAR: 1992

Few teams have been as dominant as Williams was in 1992. Its Renault-powered FW14B was in a class of its own, the engineers having produced exceptional driver aids. Nigel Mansell duly left team-mate Riccardo Patrese in his wake – and everyone else. He not only qualified on pole for the first five races but won them too. Mishaps and McLaren's Ayrton Senna were the main things between him and a clean sweep, and the title was his with five rounds still to run.

2013 DRIVERS & RESULTS

Driver	Nationality	Races	Wins	Pts	Pos
Valtteri Bottas	Finnish	19	0	4	17th
Pastor Maldonado	Venezuelan	19	0	1	18th

FOR THE RECORD

Country of origin:	England
Team base:	Grove, England
Telephone:	(44) 01235 777700
Website:	www.williamsf1.com
Active in Formula One:	From 1972
Grands Prix contested:	662
Wins:	114
Pole positions:	127
Fastest laps:	131

THE TEAM

Team principal:	Sir Frank Williams
Co-founder:	Patrick Head
Deputy team principal:	Claire Williams
Chief executive officer:	Mike O'Driscoll
Chief technical officer:	Pat Symonds
Chief designer:	Ed Wood
Head of aerodynamics:	Jason Somerville
Head of vehicle dynamics:	Rob Gearing
Chief engineer:	Xevi Pujolar
Team manager:	Dickie Stanford
Test driver:	TBA
Chassis:	Williams FW36
Engine:	Mercedes V6
Tyres:	Pirelli

engine suppliers," said Sir Frank Williams, "and we believe that they will have an extremely competitive engine package."

As well as changes under the engine cover, there has been a major change in the technical department, as Mike Coughlan left at the end of last July when the team had failed to score in the first half of the season. He was replaced by one of the most experienced technical aces in the pitlane, Pat Symonds. Down-to-earth Symonds goes all the way back to the arrival of Toleman in F1 in 1981, this being the team that went on to become Benetton and Renault and is now the Lotus F1 Team, and this long-running proximity to success will surely help Williams rediscover some of its competitiveness.

As Williams needs to reap better results to draw in more sponsorship, the death of Venezuelan president Hugo Chavez put the team into a period of nervous tension as this cast doubt on whether the considerable backing that Maldonado received from state petroleum company PDVSA would continue. Then, it was decided that they would part ways and so the impressive Valtteri Bottas will have a new team-mate in hugely experienced Ferrari refugee Felipe Massa.

Bottas did a decent job in his first season after stepping up from testing duties. He even qualified third for the Canadian GP, but the FW35 was never competitive enough for that to be maintained in the race. Indeed, he was lapped and had been demoted to 14th place by flagfall. Late in the year, he came on strong after the team ditched the Coanda exhaust and raced to eighth at the US GP.

Proudly independent, everyone wants to see Williams return to the front of the grid and Symonds will be keen to take the team forwards in the year ahead.

"The announcement of our partnership with Mercedes-Benz is exciting news for Williams. Securing the right engine supply partnership is a key milestone in the implementation of our strategy for long-term success."
Claire Williams

Claire Williams will be keen to progress after the car disappointed in her first year at the helm.

FELIPE MASSA

It was clear through the course of last season that Felipe's eight-year stint at Ferrari was coming to an end as he simply failed to add enough points to Ferrari's pot. For 2014, he has a whole new beginning after moving to Williams to lead its attack.

It's most unlikely that Felipe's move from Red Bull Racing-chasing Ferrari to Williams will be seen as a step forward, but it might just reinvigorate this affable Brazilian. Certainly, it might make him feel appreciated for the first time in years after operating very much in the shadow of Michael Schumacher, Kimi Raikkonen and then Fernando Alonso at Ferrari.

Looking at Felipe's career, it's indisputable that things have never been as good as they were before he suffered head injuries at the Hungaroring in 2009. There have been occasional flashes of his speed of old, but he has never put together a run of great performances. He has always been in Alonso's shadow since the Spaniard joined the team in 2010. Yes, there have been a number of qualifying sessions when he has ended up ahead, but he was never able to get close to Alonso's relentless attack in the races. Indeed, Felipe's lack of points across the season has had a major impact on Ferrari's eternal championship ambitions.

There might have been one more year to be had as Ferrari's loyal number

Felipe has the fresh challenge he needs for 2014 and ought to relish the opportunity.

two, but when Alonso started expressing discontent with the way things were going at Ferrari midway through last year, the team acted quickly to sign Raikkonen as a possible replacement team leader, then signed him anyway even when Alonso elected to stay.

Felipe will enjoy not having to play second fiddle to another driver, although Valtteri Bottas is held in high esteem so he may find himself with a battle on his hands again, but the chance to be valued may yet draw more from him, albeit in a less competitive car. Yet, being away from the politics of Ferrari ought to suit him well and he'll value having his experience tapped as he attempts to help this great team get back to the front again.

TRACK NOTES

Nationality:	BRAZILIAN
Born:	25 APRIL 1981, SAO PAULO, BRAZIL
Website:	www.felipemassa.com
Teams:	SAUBER 2002 & 2004-05, FERRARI 2006-13, WILLIAMS 2014

CAREER RECORD	
First Grand Prix:	2002 AUSTRALIAN GP
Grand Prix starts:	192
Grand Prix wins:	11
	2006 Turkish GP, Brazilian GP, 2007 Bahrain GP, Spanish GP, Turkish GP, 2008 Bahrain GP, Turkish GP, French GP, European GP, Belgian GP, Brazilian GP
Poles:	15
Fastest laps:	14
Points:	7044
Honours:	2008 FORMULA ONE RUNNER-UP, 2001 EUROPEAN FORMULA 3000 CHAMPION, 2000 EUROPEAN & ITALIAN FORMULA RENAULT CHAMPION, 1999 BRAZILIAN FORMULA CHEVROLET CHAMPION

NO NEED FOR FORMULA THREE

Even with the creation of GP3, Formula Three remains the key development formula for young drivers. It's the first international-level category and almost all of the greats have shone in it. Not Felipe, as he showed impressive pace in Formula Renault, winning the European and Italian titles at his first attempt. Then, buoyed by this, he simply stepped past it. Felipe didn't contest the International Formula 3000 series in 2001, but the lesser Euro series, and he won it. Then Sauber, basking in the success of plucking Kimi Raikkonen from obscurity in 2001, offered Felipe the same opportunity for 2002. He was a little wild, but his speed didn't disappoint. A year spent as Ferrari test driver in 2003 was followed by two more years with Sauber, and then his manager Nicolas Todt used his connections to land him a Ferrari ride in 2006. In 2008, Felipe was world champion for a few seconds before Lewis Hamilton landed the result he needed to pip him, and he's never been close again.

VALTTERI BOTTAS

Just four points scored in his maiden Formula One campaign may seem a fairly slim haul, but this young Finn impressed the sport's insiders last year as he knuckled down with a difficult car and delivered the goods when it finally allowed him to.

This could be a huge season for Valtteri, who started last year very much as Pastor Maldonado's number two at Williams and yet ended the season not only ahead on points but seen very much as the team's main man after the Venezuelan lost his cool and was openly critical.

Certainly, Valtteri had the complete support of the team's then executive director Toto Wolff, who had guided his career. However, the entire team seemed to be behind him too and considered him the superior talent for their future despite this being his rookie F1 campaign.

When driving a less than competitive car – and the Williams FW35 was very much one of these – you have to grasp any opportunity to shine, and Valtteri certainly did that in Canada, when it was wet for qualifying. Not only did he get through to the third qualifying session, but he was so bold in his attack on the treacherous surface that he was beaten only by Red Bull's Sebastian Vettel and Mercedes' Lewis Hamilton. In the race, in the dry, he had no hope and fell back to finish 14th, but he had laid down a marker.

It took until the last few races of the

Valtteri proved his worth by qualifying third in Canada and now needs a solid 2014.

year before Williams elected to scrap its Coanda exhaust and Valtteri suddenly found that he had a vastly better handling car and qualified ninth, with Maldonado only 17th and so rattled that he accused the team of sabotaging his car. Better still

for Valtteri, he proved that this was no fluke in the race by advancing to eighth for his first F1 points.

It was known by this point that Maldonado would be moving on, and Valtteri then found out that his partner for 2014 would be Felipe Massa. How they compare remains to be seen, but his career record shows that he definitely has raw speed, and this will surely have been augmented by the experience gained in adversity last year.

So, if Williams can be guided forward to produce a more competitive car under Pat Symonds, then Valtteri may well have a chance to put his name up in lights. The team certainly thinks that he will be capable of doing so.

TRACK NOTES

Nationality:	FINNISH
Born:	28 AUGUST 1989, NASTOLA, FINLAND
Website:	www.bottasvaltteri.com
Teams:	WILLIAMS 2013-14

CAREER RECORD

First Grand Prix:	2013 AUSTRALIAN GP
Grand Prix starts:	19
Grand Prix wins:	0
	(best result: eighth, 2013 US GP)
Poles:	0
Fastest laps:	0
Points:	4

Honours: 2011 GP3 CHAMPION, 2009 & 2010 F3 MASTERS WINNER, 2008 EUROPEAN & NORTHERN EUROPEAN FORMULA RENAULT CHAMPION, 2005 VIKING TROPHY KART WINNER

ANOTHER FLYING FINN

Following the example of earlier flying Finns JJ Lehto and Mika Hakkinen, Valtteri impressed in Scandinavian and European karting circles. His impact was soon felt when he advanced to car racing, and Valtteri became a star in Formula Renault, winning both the European title and the lesser Northern European series. His speed was clear when he stepped up to Formula Three in 2009 and not only won the Masters F3 race but ranked third in the crack European championship, behind Jules Bianchi and Christian Vietoris. His 2010 performance equalled this, as he was again third and again won the Masters race at Zandvoort. Moving on to GP3 in 2011, Valtteri became the series' second champion after Esteban Gutierrez had taken the inaugural title. At this point, he landed on Williams' books and he spent as much of 2011 as possible gaining track time in their F1 car. Impressed, Williams took him to grands prix in 2012, where he went out on track in the first Friday session.

MARUSSIA F1 TEAM

Racing with Ferrari power for the first time in 2014, the Marussia F1 Team will be pushing hard to try and move up a place in the end-of-season rankings, knowing that its survival might depend on the extra prize money that this would bring.

Jules Bianchi drove well throughout 2013 and will deliver whatever results that the latest Marussia car is capable of achieving.

The challenge of getting into Formula One is one thing, but many of the teams that have entered in the past decade have discovered that this is merely the first step and their biggest challenge has then been to find another tranche of money just to keep going. Some teams, like Super Aguri and HRT, have failed to do that. Andy Webb, the Marussia F1 Team's chief executive officer, highlighted the problem last autumn when he said, "Our investors have met with some incredulity at the way F1 costs are run. They weren't expecting to enter a spending competition, but they've put us on a solid footing and we're secure for the future." They certainly wouldn't have come into the sport expecting things to be easy, but the sheer scale of F1 spending, even at times when there are attempts being made to keep it in check, can be eye-watering.

Following the lead of the Marussia sportscar manufacturer that is the team's title sponsor, more Russian investment has been brought into the team's coffers through Andrei Chegalov. For the first time, though, Marussia will have to face up to life as not the only Russian team in F1, as Sauber now has considerable Russian backing and will be fighting Marussia to win the hearts and minds of the Russian population, a battle that will no doubt be extra intense for the first Russian GP at the new circuit in Sochi.

KEY MOMENTS AND KEY PEOPLE

JOHN BOOTH
When Virgin Racing was formed for 2010, this former Formula Ford 1600 racer was selected as team principal, as the Manor Motorsport outfit that he had built up was used as its core element. John's team had guided both Kimi Raikkonen and then Lewis Hamilton to the British Formula Renault title, then fielded Hamilton in Formula Three. It proved a good choice, and John's no-nonsense approach has guided the team through its first four campaigns, helping it to keep going forward despite a meagre budget.

GOLDEN YEAR: 2012
Coming into Formula One was a huge shock for the three new teams in 2010, and every piece of progress seemed to be exceeded by the gains made by the leading teams, but the gap is closing and this was shown in 2012 by Timo Glock racing to 12th place of the 19 finishers in Singapore. Cruelly, 10th place overall was snatched away from the team at the final round when Caterham racer Vitaly Petrov grabbed 11th place from Marussia's Charles Pic with a few laps remaining.

2013 DRIVERS & RESULTS

Driver	Nationality	Races	Wins	Pts	Pos
Jules Bianchi	French	19	0	0	19th
Max Chilton	British	19	0	0	22nd

FOR THE RECORD

Country of origin:	England
Team base:	Banbury, England
Telephone:	(44) 01909 517250
Website:	www.marussiaf1team.com
Active in Formula One:	From 2010
Grands Prix contested:	77
Wins:	0
Pole positions:	0
Fastest laps:	0

THE TEAM

Team principal:	John Booth
Chief executive officer:	Andy Webb
Sporting director:	Graeme Lowdon
Chief designer:	John McQuilliam
Deputy design chief:	Rob Taylor
Head of aerodynamics:	Richard Taylor
Head of R & D:	Richard Connell
Head of manufacturing:	Christian Silk
Chief engineer:	Dave Greenwood
Team manager:	Dave O'Neill
Chief mechanic:	Richard Wrenn
Test driver:	TBA
Chassis:	Marussia MR-03
Engine:	Ferrari V6
Tyres:	Pirelli

The biggest change for 2014 for Marussia, the team that started life in 2010 as Virgin Racing, is that it has Ferrari V6 engines powering its cars, instead of the Cosworth V8s it used before the engine regulation changes for this year. Whether this gives the team relatively more competitive engines remains to be seen, but what it certainly does do is to offer the team a glamorous association. The deal with Ferrari doesn't stop at the engines, either, as Marussia will use Ferrari energy recovery systems, transmission and ancillary systems.

A huge loss to the team last summer was the departure of Pat Symonds, who left his role as technical consultant to move on to Williams, having rehabilitated himself with Marussia following his three-year ban for his part in Renault's race-fixing debacle at the 2008 Singapore GP. This puts a lot of extra pressure on the shoulders of chief designer John McQuilliam, but he's an individual with considerable experience, having worked for Williams, Arrows and Jordan over the past quarter of a century. Supporting him, Richard Taylor brings ample experience as head of aerodynamics, as does Richard Connell as head of research and development. Their contributions are huge as they fight to find any advantage in their battle to make the team's cars faster than the Caterhams, the team with which they have spent the past few years at the tail of the grid.

A decision was taken early last autumn for Jules Bianchi to be kept on for a second year after a string of mature drives that made the most of what plainly wasn't the fastest car. The fact that he is backed by Ferrari obviously doesn't do any harm, now that there will be Ferrari V6 turbos in the rear of each of the cars.

The team's second seat, occupied last year by the well-financed Max Chilton, is set to be filled by him again.

"Last year was a character-building season. At the start, we had an advantage over Caterham, then lost ground over the middle of the year before pushing hard, catching up and enjoying some proper racing with them."

John Booth

John Booth makes sure that Marussia is the most approachable team in the F1 paddock.

JULES BIANCHI

Being supported by Ferrari certainly has its merits, as the fabled Italian race team has not only assisted Jules through the junior formulas but has now ensured that he will enjoy a second year of his Formula One apprenticeship with Marussia.

Jules landed his Formula One break at the 11th hour last year when Ferrari put him into the second seat at Marussia in place of Timo Glock, bringing a budget to ease his entry to this financially restricted team and so move the experienced Glock towards touring car racing. Jules is certainly a driver who could go places, having displayed speed aplenty on the way up towards F1, and last year, his first in the World Championship, he did everything that was expected of him.

In some ways, learning their craft with a team at the back of the grid enables drivers to stay "under the radar", to have the chance to build up their experience and earn those oh so valuable track miles before hopefully being given a shot with one of the teams under the main spotlight if they've done well. If they make any mistakes, then they're not so obvious.

This certainly seemed to serve Jules well last year, as he knuckled down to learn the circuits beyond Europe that he didn't get to learn when he raced in GP2 and Formula Renault 3.5. He had the beating of fellow F1 rookie Max Chilton and

Jules is back for more, after a rookie year in which his promise was masked by the car.

displayed a cool head in races, something that wasn't always apparent on his way up the racing ladder when he squandered points finishes in the heat of battle, most notably in GP2 in 2010 and 2011.

Team principal John Booth was impressed, saying, "Jules rose to the challenge of the season exceptionally well and since that time has clearly demonstrated his ability and potential."

Emphasizing its confidence in Jules's ability, and making plain its new connection with Ferrari, Marussia announced before last year's Korean GP that he would be staying for a second season.

How Jules fares in the year ahead is linked entirely to how competitive Marussia can make its new-style car. If he wants to land a top drive, he can only afford one more year with a tail end team before a move up the ranks becomes essential for his career.

TRACK NOTES

Nationality:	FRENCH
Born:	3 AUGUST 1989, NICE, FRANCE
Website:	www.jules-bianchi.com
Teams:	MARUSSIA 2013-14

CAREER RECORD

First Grand Prix:	2013 AUSTRALIAN GP
Grand Prix starts:	19
Grand Prix wins:	0
(best result: 13th, 2013 Malaysian GP)	
Poles:	0
Fastest laps:	0
Points:	0
Honours:	2012 FORMULA RENAULT 3.5 RUNNER-UP, 2011 GP2 ASIA RUNNER-UP, 2009 EUROPEAN FORMULA THREE CHAMPION, 2008 ELF MASTERS FORMULA THREE WINNER, 2007 FRENCH FORMULA RENAULT CHAMPION

GUIDED FORWARDS BY FERRARI

Racing runs in Jules's bloodline, as his great-grandfather moved from Italy to Belgium to run Johnny Claes's racing exploits, then both his grandfather Mauro and his great-uncle Lucien became racing drivers. Lucien not only raced in F1, finishing third at Monaco for Cooper in 1968, but won that year's Le Mans 24 Hours with Ford. A year later, he died testing for the same event. Jules showed promise in Formula Renault then F3, winning the European title with ART Grand Prix in 2009, at which point Ferrari signed him up as a star for the future, allowing him an F1 test. A frontrunner in GP2 with ART Grand Prix in 2010 and 2011, ranking third overall each year, Jules moved to the Formula Renault 3.5 series with Tech 1 Racing in 2012 and won three times across the 17 rounds to finish the year as runner-up, pipped by Robin Frijns. Jules remains part of the Ferrari Driver Academy, but gained F1 test experience with Force India before a very late deal landed a season of gaining F1 racing experience with Marussia in 2013.

MAX CHILTON*

Max was never going to win races or even score World Championship points in his rookie Formula One season. He did, however, bring his car home in each of the 19 grands prix. This year, he'll just be hoping that he can build on that experience.

When racing for Marussia, drivers have to be realistic and accept that they will spend the whole of the year scrapping for position outside the point-scoring places and that a top-10 finish will come their way only in a race of unusual attrition. They know too that their rare appearances on television will inevitably be when their car is coming up to be lapped rather than pulling off a stunning overtaking manoeuvre. Their endeavours are thus spotted only by those who examine the timing screens closely during a grand prix and can thus check on their performance. Thus, a mighty drive to 18th place could easily go all but unnoticed, but it could be their best performance of the whole year.

Indeed, the most easily recalled moment of Max's rookie F1 season in 2013 was his unfortunate clash with Pastor Maldonado's Williams during the Monaco GP that brought the race to a temporary halt while the track was cleared. Yet, the Marussia team appreciated his efforts. Sure, he was generally eclipsed by team-mate Jules Bianchi, a driver with more F1 test runs beneath his belt before the opening round.

Max's main target for 2014 will once more be his own team-mate, Jules Bianchi.

However, Max didn't make many mistakes, made genuine strides after the summer break and will have gained considerable experience from finishing each of the 19 races; for, in these days of almost no testing during the season, track time is everything.

Of course, as Max goes into his second season with Marussia, talk will continue of him being a pay-driver, but the tail end teams wouldn't survive without them. Now he must show that he has gained from competing on circuits last year that he had never visited previously and step up his pace in the season ahead.

Perhaps the key to Max's performances in 2014 will be the confidence that he gained through the course of last season as much as any comparative performance gain that Marussia might manage against arch-rivals Caterham.

Team principal John Booth points out that although Max looks angelic he has a core of steel, and this will clearly be required again in 2014 as he and Bianchi try again not to be last home from the back row of the grid.

TRACK NOTES

Nationality:	BRITISH
Born:	21 APRIL 1991, REIGATE, ENGLAND
Website:	www.maxchilton.com
Teams:	MARUSSIA 2013-14

CAREER RECORD

First Grand Prix:	2013 AUSTRALIAN GP
Grand Prix starts:	19
Grand Prix wins:	0
	(best result: 14th, 2013 Monaco GP)
Poles:	0
Fastest laps:	0
Points:	0
Honours:	2006 T-CAR RUNNER-UP

RACING CARS FROM THE AGE OF 14

Max was an early starter in motor racing as he didn't stay the course in karting. Instead he opted to step up to cars as soon as he could, advancing to the T-Car series, in which drivers as young as 14 can race silhouette saloon cars, just as his elder brother Tom had done before him. Second overall in his second year, Max then tried a variety of series in 2007, racing in Pro Mazda in the USA, but also trying British F3 and sportscars in the Le Mans Series. For 2008, he focused on British F3, and then made progress when he joined Carlin in 2009 and ranked fourth in a season dominated by Daniel Ricciardo. Having tried the more powerful GP2 in the Asian series, he had a full campaign in 2010, but it was only in his third year of GP2, with Carlin in 2012, that he started winning, and his fourth place overall plus his considerable family financial backing landed Max his F1 break for 2013.

* unconfirmed at time of going to press.

Valtteri Bottas came on strong during his first year racing for Williams and ended the season with more points than team-mate Pastor Maldonado.

CATERHAM F1 TEAM

This team has spent four campaigns since joining the World Championship running around at or near the tail of the field. It needs to reduce its deficit to the midfield teams by 2s per lap if it's to rise up the order. It's a considerable ask.

Giedo van der Garde went increasingly well during 2013, but Caterham was unlikely to score points with two rookie drivers.

It was clear last year that Caterham had far from the most competitive car on the grid. Indeed, it usually had only Marussia to play with as this pair of teams that entered Formula One together in 2010 vied not to be slowest of all. While Caterham usually came out ahead, the relative speed of the Marussias may have had a negative effect on Caterham's form for the season ahead, as it forced the design team to continue developing the 2013 car past the point when it had planned to turn its attention to developing the radically changed car and engine combination required by this year's new rules.

One matter that may have slowed the team slightly last year was running two rookie drivers and this is why the return of Heikki Kovalainen after a year spent on the sidelines was hinted at by team owner Tony Fernandes, who said that he wanted a driver with more experience than either F1 sophomore Charles Pic or rookie Giedo van der Garde could offer last year. "It's no secret that I'm close to Heikki and I have a lot of time for him," said the Malaysian entrepreneur last autumn. "Certainly, the driver who won the Hungarian GP for McLaren in 2008 has plenty to offer." His re-employment is a clear sign that the team is doing everything in its power in its attempt to move away from the tail of the grid, something that is hugely

KEY MOMENTS AND KEY PEOPLE

JOHN ILEY

Even when studying at Imperial College, John's work had a motor racing angle to it as he worked on data analysis and wind tunnel testing. His first job was with Brun, working on the EuroBrun F1 car and then on a sports-prototype racer. He then produced the Allard sportscar before returning to F1 with Jordan in 1995. He moved to Renault in 2002, following technical director Mike Gascoyne. Then, two years later, he went to Ferrari as chief aerodynamicist, later performing the same role for McLaren, then Caterham.

GOLDEN YEAR: 2012

With this young team having not yet scored a World Championship point, it may be premature to pick out a golden year, but 2012 marked something of a breakthrough as Heikki Kovalainen and Vitaly Petrov gave chase to the more established teams. The Finn's 13th place at Monaco was useful in moving the team against its other non-scoring colleagues, but it was the Russian's 11th place in the final round that clinched the lucrative 10th place in the team rankings.

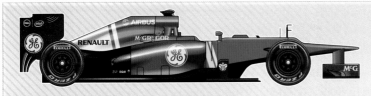

2013 DRIVERS & RESULTS

Driver	Nationality	Races	Wins	Pts	Pos
Charles Pic	French	19	0	0	20th
Giedo van der Garde	Dutch	19	0	0	21st

FOR THE RECORD

Country of origin:	England
Team base:	Leafield, England
Telephone:	(44) 01953 851411
Website:	www.caterhamf1.com
Active in Formula One:	From 2010
Grands Prix contested:	77
Wins:	0
Pole positions:	0
Fastest laps:	0

THE TEAM

Team owners:	Tony Fernandes & Dato-Kamarudin Meranun
Chief executive officer:	Graham Macdonald
Team principal:	Cyril Abiteboul
Technical director:	Mark Smith
Deputy technical director:	Jody Egginton
Performance director:	John Iley
Chief designer:	Lewis Butler
Head of aerodynamics:	Hari Roberts
Head of R&D:	Elliot Dason-Barber
Team manager:	Graham Watson
Chief engineer:	Gianluca Pisanello
Test driver:	TBA
Chassis:	Caterham CT04
Engine:	Renault V6
Tyres:	Pirelli

significant when the team prize money is handed out at the end of the season, with the team ranked last receiving nothing.

Van der Garde held on to the team's second seat and ought to benefit from having the Finn as team-mate. Of course, as the team's reserve driver last year Heikki was around at races, but having his views on how the car handles is of even more use when he's been out in the same session.

Caterham will continue to use Renault engines until the end of 2016, hoping no doubt that the Renault Energy F1 V6 turbo is just as competitive as its normally aspirated V8 predecessor was. This continuation was expected as Caterham Cars signed a joint venture agreement with Renault's Alpine brand in late 2012 to develop a new range of lightweight road cars. With the company expanding fast, looking into building an SUV and entering Moto 2 motorbike racing, Caterham Cars' CEO Graham Macdonald has expanded his role to take in the running of the F1 team as well.

Last autumn, the Leafield-based team's technical department was restructured, with Jody Egginton promoted from operations director to deputy technical director. With his strong engineering background – Jody joined the team at its inception as chief engineer – his move helped to free up technical director Mark Smith as Caterham focused on developing this year's car. Performance director John Iley has had his remit broadened to manage Caterham's Advanced Projects Group.

Pic and van der Garde took time to get going last year as Caterham's CT02 found its feet. Although development parts were introduced, the fact that neither driver managed to score meant that it and Marussia would be ranked according to their best placing. But Pic's 14th place at Sepang was not enough to see it 10th overall as Jules Bianchi had finished 13th in the same race, thus enabling Marussia to claim the final share of the season's prize fund.

"The depth of our partnership with Renault will certainly pay dividends this year, helping to give us the best opportunity to continue our progress up the grid in 2014 and beyond."

Cyril Abiteboul

Cyril Abiteboul will now be answerable to Caterham Cars' CEO Graham Macdonald.

HEIKKI KOVALAINEN*

Heikki was being lined up to rejoin Caterham for 2014 when he was given two outings for Lotus and found it harder to step in than he had expected. However, Tony Fernandes still values the experience that he can bring.

Heikki has had a strangely convoluted Formula One career – he's driven for two teams called Lotus for starters – and signing for a full campaign with the Caterham F1 Team is the first step towards putting it back on track.

This is still a team attempting to fight its way clear of the back of the grid, still chipping away at the seconds between it and the top teams as it lines up ahead of its fifth year of F1. It's certainly a long way back from the Renault team Heikki raced for in his rookie F1 campaign in 2007 and his team for the next two years, McLaren. Yet Caterham is a team that values his experience and knows that he can win if offered competitive equipment, as he proved in Hungary in 2008 when he won for McLaren.

60

After a year spent largely on the sidelines as Caterham's reserve driver there was a chance to show his speed when he was offered the attractive proposition of two race outings for Lotus, who needed a stand-in for Kimi Raikkonen when he had to miss the final two rounds to have back surgery. Heikki had the advantage

Caterham is looking to Heikki again for his experience as well as for his speed.

of knowing many of the team personnel, remaining from his previous spell with the team back in 2007 when it was called Renault. However, having no track time ahead of the first practice session cost

him dearly, and he failed to collect points either in the USA or Brazil, trailing home 14th in both races.

Putting this disappointment aside, Heikki has a big fan in Caterham owner Tony Fernandes and knows that he is much valued for the experience that he can bring and hopefully use to good effect to harness all the speed available, not just from this year's Caterham CT04 but also from his less experienced team-mate as Caterham chases those vital points.

TRACK NOTES

Nationality:	FINNISH
Born:	19 OCTOBER 1981, SUOMUSSALMI, FINLAND
Website:	www.heikkikovalainen.net
Teams:	RENAULT 2007, McLAREN 2008-09, LOTUS/CATERHAM 2010-12, LOTUS 2013, CATERHAM 2014

CAREER RECORD	
First Grand Prix:	2007 AUSTRALIAN GP
Grand Prix starts:	111
Grand Prix wins:	1
	2008 Hungarian GP
Poles:	1
Fastest laps:	2
Points:	105
Honours:	2005 GP2 RUNNER-UP, 2004 FORMULA NISSAN WORLD SERIES CHAMPION & CHAMPION OF CHAMPIONS AT THE RACE OF CHAMPIONS, 2003 FORMULA NISSAN WORLD SERIES RUNNER-UP, 2000 NORDIC KARTING CHAMPION

OPTING FOR RACING, NOT RALLYING

Almost every one of Heikki's contemporaries at Suomussalmi would have thought first of rallying, as dirt roads abounded around them. Heikki went karting instead, landing the Nordic title when he was 18. He then headed to race in British Formula Renault in 2001 and he impressed on circuits he'd never seen before, ranking fourth. Stepping up to Formula Three in 2002, he came third in the British championship. He then raced in World Series by Nissan and was runner-up before landing the title in 2004. This led to F1 tests with Renault, and he did some more in 2005 when he raced to second overall in GP2 behind Nico Rosberg. What gained him considerable fame was winning the 2004 Race of Champions tournament ahead of Michael Schumacher. After another year of testing, Heikki made his F1 debut in 2007. McLaren took him on and he won in Hungary in 2008, but with Lewis Hamilton dominating the team he moved to the new Lotus team in 2010, staying until 2012, when it had become Caterham.

* unconfirmed at time of going to press.

GIEDO VAN DER GARDE*

Giedo deserves a second shot at Formula One as he showed marked improvement through his rookie campaign with the Caterham F1 Team, and he is expected to occupy the team's second seat again, this time alongside a more experienced driver.

With the final seats for 2014 taking a while to be sorted during last winter, stories surfaced that Marcel Boekhoorn, the father of Giedo's fiancée, might use his considerable wealth to invest either in Force India or Williams, and thus land Giedo a drive for 2014. However, Giedo dashed those rumours immediately, saying that he was hoping to continue with Caterham but was also talking to other teams, also pointing out that his future father-in-law would be able to afford only a minority stake in either of those teams, meaning that he wouldn't be able to force the team's hand on driver selection anyway.

In the end, a return to Caterham looked most likely, and Giedo feels more than prepared to give an even better account of himself if he lands it, especially as the team wants to have an experienced hand in the lead seat after perhaps not doing as well as it could last year, when Charles Pic was its lead driver despite having only one year's worth of F1 racing behind him.

In 2013 there was certainly a culture shock at first for Giedo, who pointed out that he had gone from a team of 15 people in GP2 to one with more than 200.

Giedo got quicker during his rookie F1 season and wants to make his mark in 2014.

What the then 28-year-old Dutchman also found hard was the way that last year's Caterham CT03 used its tyres and found that he was driving too aggressively to make them last. It took him half a season before his improved understanding of this element of car performance, as well as upgrades to the car and Pirelli changing back to 2012 tyre compounds, let him show his true pace.

The biggest gain wasn't in qualifying, in which he usually matched Pic, but in the races themselves, with his 14th-place finish in the Hungarian GP his top result before a run of clashes in late-season events spoiled some of his outings.

Giedo's most high-profile moment, though, came in the Belgian GP at Spa-Francorchamps, where a gamble to try slicks on a wet track helped him to third place in the first qualifying session. The drying track meant that he would start the race 14th, but he had made the most of this rare opportunity to put his name up in lights.

TRACK NOTES

Nationality:	DUTCH
Born:	25 APRIL 1985, RHENEN, HOLLAND
Website:	www.giedovandergarde.com
Teams:	CATERHAM 2013-14

CAREER RECORD

First Grand Prix:	2013 AUSTRALIAN GP
Grand Prix starts:	19
Grand Prix wins:	0 (best result: 14th, 2013 Hungarian GP)
Poles:	0
Fastest laps:	0
Points:	0
Honours:	2008 FORMULA RENAULT 3.5 CHAMPION, 2002 WORLD KART CHAMPION, 1988 DUTCH KART CHAMPION

PLAYING THE LONG GAME

Giedo was World Kart Champion in the Super A category in 2002 and then moved up to cars, racing in Formula Renault in 2003. He advanced to Formula Three and was the second best rookie in the 2004 European championship. Two more seasons resulted in just one win and a best ranking of sixth in 2006, when Paul di Resta beat Sebastian Vettel to the title. Then Giedo stepped up to Formula Renault 3.5 and ranked sixth in that, but the highlight of his year was his first taste of Formula One with test runs for Super Aguri and Spyker. In 2008, Giedo landed the Renault 3.5 title, five places ahead of his future F1 team-mate Charles Pic. Giedo got a taste of GP2 in the 2008/09 Asian winter series before racing in the main championship for the next three years, during which time he had further F1 tests with Force India, Renault and Caterham. Fifth overall in 2011, Giedo failed to get his F1 break, so he stayed in GP2 in 2012, and this time after ranking sixth he got his opportunity.

* unconfirmed at time of going to press.

TALKING POINT: FORMULA ONE REVERTS TO TURBO ENGINES

There's an F1 engine revolution in 2014 as all teams must use a new, smaller engine. Engine capacity is reduced to 1600cc, but this won't mean less power as units are turbocharged and boosted with energy recovery systems.

Formula One is hit periodically by rule changes dictating that teams must fit a new type of engine, and this year heralds the arrival of the eighth new capacity or type of engine in the 65 years of the World Championship. After an eight-year reign, the 2.4-litre V8 engines that themselves were a reduction in size and the number of cylinders from their predecessors have been consigned to history.

When it was announced back in July 2011 that engines were going to be reduced to 1.6 litres, the natural reaction was one of horror, as fans thought that this would emasculate the sport's top category. Yet, the manufacturers soon reckoned that the turbocharged V6 units would be able to push out just as much power as their normally aspirated V8s had, at around 750bhp, and offer more torque to make them more driveable. To achieve this, the new V6s would have to be far more fuel-efficient, something that would be dictated by the 100kg (around 140 litres) per hour fuel flow they'll be permitted. This is a limiting factor, but it's in keeping with the savings the automotive manufacturers are finding on their road cars as they produce smaller engines and use fewer revs, and it's something that the sport's governing body is keen to be seen to be achieving with F1.

"The performance is going to come from the thermal efficiency of the engine relative to the chemical energy that goes in," explains Rob White of Renault Sport F1. To achieve this, he said, the first target would be to maximize the piston energy and minimize the energy in the exhaust.

One factor that will actually be increased for 2014 is the amount of power gain when using energy recovery systems, and this will be allowed to be used for a greater length of time each lap. One of the major differences from before is that the new system, known as ERS, will use the retrieval of heat energy as well as kinetic energy, and it's expected to offer the drivers a boost of 120kW, double what KERS did, which translates to an extra 160bhp. Better still, the drivers will be allowed this for up to 33.3s per lap, thanks to a greater storage facility, as opposed to last year's 6.7s limit.

The engineers have suggested that while it would have been difficult to be quick without KERS in 2013, it would be impossible to go racing without ERS in 2014.

The hard stats of the new engine compared to the old one is that it's 800cc smaller and is allowed 3,000 revs fewer, capped at 15,000rpm. Its minimum weight, with ERS, is 145kg, up 50kg on the old engine, not counting its KERS. Engine life will be doubled, from 2,000km to 4,000km, and each driver will be allowed five engines per year rather than last year's eight.

Regardless of the power pushed out, many F1 fans and even a few of the drivers were concerned that the new engines might sound weedy. F1 impresario Bernie Ecclestone was less than impressed when he first heard one run on a dyno late in 2012, calling its sound "terrible". The engine

note isn't as loud but it's higher pitched, and Andy Cowell, the man in charge of Mercedes' F1 engines, responded by saying, "The V6 turbos are loud, but I think sweeter sounding."

Multiple World Champion Sebastian Vettel was among the doubters, saying last September, "I think F1 needs to be loud. It has to make a lot of noise and have a lot of power. In 2014, at peak power maybe we will have even more power than in 2013, but it will be lacking a couple of cylinders."

Adrian Sutil stressed the point even more, saying, "I'd like to say that I'm looking forward to a V12 ..."

Any regulation change offers the opportunity for a team or manufacturer to find an advantage, but Red Bull's Vettel isn't worried. "I believe that the top teams will still be ahead," said the German. "The only question is in what order. It's always the same in F1 as everything is mixed up before it stabilizes again." Cowell reckons that the rule change gives the manufacturers more scope to make their mark than before, using the slogan "We're putting the motor back in motor racing."

Ferrari, Mercedes and Renault are all building engines for this new formula, and their number will be bolstered in 2015 when Honda returns to team up with McLaren for the first time since 1992.

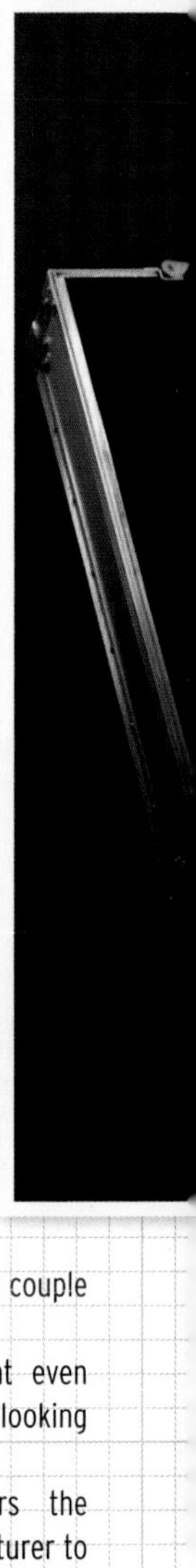

Right: Ayrton Senna was one of the stars of the first turbo era. He's shown here in his Lotus at the 1986 French GP at Paul Ricard, holding off Nigel Mansell's Williams.

Left: Smaller and more compact than the 2013 V8 engines, this turbocharged Renault F1 V6 is the shape of things to come. Engine designers have spent since 2011 developing them to ensure that they can return fuel savings of a third over their predecessors.

Below: Flame-outs on the over-run were a feature of the 1980s, but this blaze from the rear of Stefan Johansson's Ferrari in qualifying for the 1986 Italian GP is even more spectacular and shows that the team had gone for too much turbo boost and his engine has let go.

TALKING POINT:
HOW SEBASTIAN VETTEL
RANKS IN F1 HISTORY

Sebastian Vettel's remarkable four Formula One titles in succession with Red Bull Racing have propelled him from being a one-time grand prix winner in 2008 with Scuderia Toro Rosso to a serious record-breaker.

It all started at Monza in 2008, a very wet Monza, when Sebastian was in his first full season of Formula One after a handful of races first for BMW Sauber then Scuderia Toro Rosso in 2007. He was kept on by the Italian team and not only gave it its first pole position but was never headed in the race and gave it its first win.

This helped him to land promotion to Red Bull Racing, the senior partner in Red Bull's F1 empire. As it happens, Red Bull Racing had been embarrassed by its feeder team Toro Rosso beating it to score a win, but its own first victory came soon enough, when Sebastian won the third race of 2009, the Chinese GP. He then added three further wins, at Silverstone, Suzuka and Yas Marina, to rank second overall behind Jenson Button, who had enjoyed a superior car as Brawn GP had utilized double diffuser technology to garner an advantage.

Since then, it has been Sebastian all the way and by the end of the 2013 season, when he had clinched his fourth F1 title in a row, he had become, at the age of 26, the third most titled driver ever, behind Michael Schumacher (seven F1 titles) and Juan Manuel Fangio (five). Only Schumacher has scored more titles in succession, with his run of five in a row for Ferrari between 2000 and 2004.

Another relatively rare feat that he had achieved was following up his first F1 title with another the following year, something achieved before only by Alberto Ascari for Ferrari in 1953, Jack Brabham for Cooper in 1960, Alain Prost for McLaren in 1986, Schumacher for Benetton in 1995, Mika Hakkinen for McLaren in 1999 and Fernando

Alonso for Renault in 2006. Certainly, Sebastian had the benefit of being with a team that kept its form, but he still had to beat his team-mate, Mark Webber, to take the wins needed to claim these titles.

Qualifying on pole position is something of a weapon in his arsenal, most notably in 2011 when he was on pole for 15 of the 19 rounds, and Sebastian had done this 45 times by the end of last year, cementing his position of third in the all-time chart that continues to be led by Schumacher on 68, from Ayrton Senna on 65.

Recording the fastest lap of a grand prix has never been a key ingredient to being first to the chequered flag, especially in the largely tactical races of the past few years, as drivers have had to not only nurse their tyres but also watch their fuel consumption since refuelling was banned at the end of 2009. Sebastian has 22 of these, a relatively paltry collection considering that his more experienced compatriot Schumacher gathered 76, albeit after contesting 308 grands prix to Sebastian's 120. Prost and Kimi Raikkonen rank second and third on 41 and 39 respectively.

Schumacher is still way out front in terms of wins, too, his tally of 91 unlikely to be beaten, unless Sebastian remains in tandem with ace designer Adrian Newey. By the end of last year, Sebastian ranked fourth in the all-time wins list, with 39. His next target is Senna's tally of 41 victories.

His 13 wins from last year's 19 rounds moves him equal top of the table for the most wins in a season, matching Michael Schumacher's record set with Ferrari back in 2004.

Schumacher also tops the table for laps led, on 5,111, but Sebastian passed Scottish greats Jackie Stewart and Jim Clark, then Nigel Mansell as well last year as he advanced to 2,437 to lie fourth of all time behind Schumacher, Senna (2,987) and Prost (2,684).

The recent change in the number of points awarded for a win to 25 means that Sebastian remains third overall, as he was at the end of last year, but has advanced to 1,451, moving him ever closer to Schumacher (1,566 points) and new table-topper Alonso (1,606), with the greats of earlier decades receiving less than half of that for being first to the chequered flag.

Of course, the ever greater number of grands prix held each year these days also means that these figures are skewed in favour of drivers competing in the 21st century rather than in the 1950s and 1960s, but however one looks at it Sebastian's ascent of these charts has been quite remarkably fast.

Right: Michael Schumacher marks the end of his remarkable F1 career after the 2012 Brazilian GP by congratulating the driver who one day might surpass all of his F1 records: Sebastian Vettel.

Below: Ayrton Senna claimed three world titles before his untimely death at Imola in 1994. Here, he celebrates the last of his wins, at Adelaide in the final race of 1993.

Above: Juan Manuel Fangio was the driver who set the standards in the 1950s. Here the great Argentinian races to victory at the Nurburgring in 1957 in his works Maserati.

Sebastian Vettel powers past Lewis Hamilton up the hill to Les Combes on the opening lap of the Belgian GP, the start of a run of nine wins.

KNOW THE TRACKS 2014

The shape of the Formula One calendar continues to chop and change. India and Korea have been dropped, Austria returns and Russia makes its bow but the proposed events in Mexico and New Jersey will now have to wait to join the show. Altogether, there will be 19 grands prix in 2014.

The World Championship has undergone considerable flux in the 21st century. The modus operandi of the sport's promoters has been to push Formula One to countries to which it has never ventured before, thus the grands prix of China, Korea and India. However, not all of these have proved hits, with crowds still disappointing in China and Korea, and an excess of bureaucracy stifling the race in India. Yet, in their wake, Russia's long-awaited debut in the World Championship is now upon us and promises a race already publicized by the Sochi Winter Olympics.

The flow of the championship starts with the now established opening round in Australia. As usual, it is followed by the Malaysian GP, but they are no longer a pair, with a two-week gap between them and the race at Sepang now part of a two-race set with the Bahrain GP the following Sunday, this time being run under floodlights after dark to fit in with TV viewing times for the prime European market. Then, after another fortnight, the fourth round will be the Chinese GP held as usual outside Shanghai.

The "European season", when the teams can drive all their equipment and giant hospitality centres to the circuits rather than airfreight a minimal amount of kit to the flyaway events, starts as usual in Spain, a country that is now accustomed to hosting only one grand prix per year since the demise of the European

GP on the Valencia street circuit after 2012. Monaco comes next. Then, after a dash across the Atlantic to Montreal for the Canadian GP, the season has an interesting new addition: the Austrian GP. This is an event that has not been held since 2003, after which the A1-Ring fell into disrepair. Now owned by Red Bull, the circuit has been restored and renamed the Red Bull Ring and it will bring a dose of beautiful scenery (the Styrian mountains form a dramatic backdrop) to TV audiences once more.

Silverstone, now on a much more sound financial footing, continues to host the British GP, which heralds the start of the regular sequence of races, meaning that it's followed by Germany (Hockenheim this time, as the race alternates with Nurburgring), Hungary, Belgium and Italy.

The night race in Singapore follows as before, after which there is again a two-week gap, but following the dropping of the Korean GP, the Japanese GP is now next up.

The race at Suzuka has a new partner as it's paired with this year's only all-new race: the Russian GP. This is a major undertaking, as it's going to be held on an all-new circuit built in and around the central facility of Sochi's base for the Olympic Winter Games. The major unknown while this season was being planned last year was whether the circuit would be ready in time for its October date, with the Winter Games due to continue until 23 February, making it impossible for much of the construction work to be started until after that, which is why some suggested that this race's debut might be delayed by 12 months.

Rejigging the calendar at the start of last December, when the 2014 programme was cut back from the provisional 22 grands prix to 19, led to a major reshaping of the end-of-season races. Since the proposed return of the Mexican GP, on the list of maybes for the first time since 1992, came to nothing, there is now a North America-South America double-header, with a visit to the Circuit of the Americas in Texas followed seven days later by the year's penultimate race at Interlagos in Brazil. Thus, 2014 will have a new season-closing event, as the Abu Dhabi GP has now claimed that slot, again as a twilight event, with a double allocation of points up for grabs.

The proposed race that fell by the wayside that will be most missed will be the one that really would have taken F1 to a new audience. It was the one that F1 supremo Bernie Ecclestone craves, a grand prix in New York. A street layout was selected just across the river at Hoboken in New Jersey but the new facility could not be made ready in time.

Nineteen races, rather than 22, will suit the teams better on a technical issue. They pointed out that the new engines were good for four races only and with the teams being allowed five engines per driver, this meant a maximum of 20 races.

MELBOURNE

There will be no Mark Webber for the local fans to cheer this year, so it's a good thing that fellow Australian racer Daniel Ricciardo has stepped up to take his place at Red Bull Racing.

When compared to classic circuits of the standard of Spa-Francorchamps, Suzuka and Silverstone, Melbourne's Albert Park falls short, yet that's not for want of effort. It's simply that it doesn't have either the topography or the high-speed corners to match the excitement that these long-standing tracks supply.

Yet, what it does have is the excitement of hosting the season's opening grand prix, which is the first chance for F1 fans and of course the teams to find out how things stack up for the campaign ahead. This fact alone makes Albert Park a great place to be, while in addition the race programme is one of the most packed with support races anywhere in the world. Australians certainly know how to run world-class sports events.

The circuit, located in a city park, starts with a bang as there is often a collision or two at the opening corner. If not there, then down at Turn 3, an even tighter righthander. From there, the lap is slow and scratchy until it rounds the far corner of the lake and finds its flow, especially through the arcing section from Turn 9 to Turn 13, Ascari, although Turn 11 presents a test with its blind entry. The rest of the lap is a sequence of slow corners, but throw in sunshine and the season could not have a better place to start.

"I can't say that Albert Park is my favourite track, but I love coming to Australia, which is a great country with very nice people who really like their racing." **Felipe Massa**

INSIDE TRACK
AUSTRALIAN GRAND PRIX

Date:	**16 March**
Circuit name:	**Albert Park**
Circuit length:	**3.295 miles/5.300km**
Number of laps:	**58**
Email:	**enquiries@grandprix.com.au**
Website:	**www.grandprix.com.au**

PREVIOUS WINNERS		
2004	**Michael Schumacher**	FERRARI
2005	**Giancarlo Fisichella**	RENAULT
2006	**Fernando Alonso**	RENAULT
2007	**Kimi Raikkonen**	FERRARI
2008	**Lewis Hamilton**	McLAREN
2009	**Jenson Button**	BRAWN
2010	**Jenson Button**	McLAREN
2011	**Sebastian Vettel**	RED BULL
2012	**Jenson Button**	McLAREN
2013	**Kimi Raikkonen**	LOTUS

F1 in Australia: Adelaide won the right to host the World Championship on its temporary street layout in 1985. This was a huge success, but in 1996 the race was wrested away by the financial clout of Melbourne, where it has stayed ever since.

Most successful Australian driver: Alan Jones's father Stan won the Australian GP in 1959 when it was still a local event. Alan himself went several steps better and became World Champion for Williams in 1980. Even this, though, did not compare with Jack Brabham's record of three F1 titles, two with Cooper in 1959 and 1960, then another with his own team in 1966.

Best corner: Turn 11, the tightish lefthander with a blind entry, breaks up the flow of the fast stretch around the far side of Albert Park's lake.

Location: When Melbourne won the rights to host the Australian GP, it did so by agreeing to build a temporary circuit in a park about a mile to the south of the city centre. With tram routes running along all four sides of the park, access is easier than to other circuits. The park has benefited enormously from the investment the race organizers have had to make to modernize its other facilities as part of its deal for racing there.

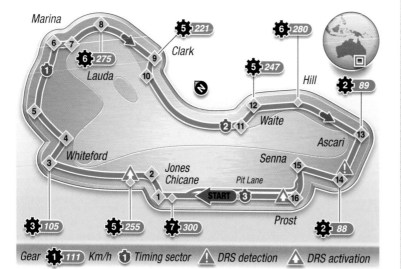

2013 POLE TIME: **VETTEL (RED BULL),**
1M27.407S, 135.710MPH/218.404KPH
2013 WINNER'S AVERAGE SPEED:
127.335MPH/204.926KPH

2013 FASTEST LAP: **RAIKKONEN (LOTUS),**
1M29.274S, 132.883MPH/213.855KPH
LAP RECORD: **M. SCHUMACHER (FERRARI),**
1M24.125S, 141.016MPH/226.944KPH, 2004

SEPANG

This is a circuit that offers plenty of opportunity for overtaking and where over the years the added factor of the sudden arrival of torrential rain has been thrown in to spice up the proceedings.

When Hermann Tilke penned the Sepang circuit, to be hewn from the jungle to the south of capital Kuala Lumpur, he gave it the sort of flow that drivers adore, and they have responded since its inaugural grand prix in 1999 with some fabulous racing action.

A lap here starts in spectacular fashion as the long start/finish straight ends with a wide entry into a righthand hairpin that is the first part of a two-corner sequence, and drivers can choose a number of lines both in and out of it.

If a driver can execute a good exit from Turn 2 and gain ground through the arc of Turn 3, then Turn 4, a tight right over a crest, can be another place to try a move. The esse of Turns 5/6 is for the brave, as is Turn 12, before the lap concludes with another long straight into a tight corner, this one a simple hairpin and definitely a possible passing place.

One factor that greatly concerns the teams and most especially the drivers is the weather. It's never less than extremely hot, as you would expect in the tropics, but this is made more draining still by often soaring humidity. Rain plays a big part here too, often coming in both fast and heavy, making the timing of a qualifying run or a mid-race change of tyres all the more critical.

"If the car is quick and stable, you can enjoy it, but sometimes you really struggle for balance at Sepang and then it's a real challenge as the corners are so long." **Adrian Sutil**

INSIDE TRACK
MALAYSIAN GRAND PRIX

Date:	**30 March**
Circuit name:	**Sepang Circuit**
Circuit length:	**3.444 miles/5.542km**
Number of laps:	**56**
Email:	inquiries@sepangcircuit.com.my
Website:	www.malaysiangp.com.my

PREVIOUS WINNERS

2004	**Michael Schumacher** FERRARI
2005	**Fernando Alonso** RENAULT
2006	**Giancarlo Fisichella** RENAULT
2007	**Fernando Alonso** McLAREN
2008	**Kimi Raikkonen** FERRARI
2009	**Jenson Button** BRAWN
2010	**Sebastian Vettel** RED BULL
2011	**Sebastian Vettel** RED BULL
2012	**Fernando Alonso** FERRARI
2013	**Sebastian Vettel** RED BULL

F1 in Malaysia: Street races were held in Malaysia and neighbouring Singapore in the 1960s, but the first permanent circuit wasn't built until the mid-1980s, at Selangor, which hosted a round of the World Endurance Championship in 1985. Malaysia's big breakthrough was the construction of Sepang, with a grand prix following from 1999.

Most successful Malaysian driver: Alex Yoong is the only Malaysian to have raced in Formula One thus far, competing for Minardi from late 2001 to 2002. He failed to shine for this tailend team, but did better by winning races for the Malaysian team in A1GP in 2005/06. The next in line for Formula One is Jazeman Jaafar, who raced strongly in Formula Renault 3.5 last year.

Best corner: Turn 12 edges Turn 5 as the toughest of the lap, with drivers aiming to take this testing lefthand kink at around 160mph in sixth gear and hang on sufficiently around this slightly downhill bend to be able to turn in to Turn 13.

Location: Access to Kuala Lumpur's airport was always going to be vital for Malaysia's premier circuit, and a site was duly selected in a shallow valley in the tropical jungle just two miles to the north of the runways, 30 miles south of the capital.

71

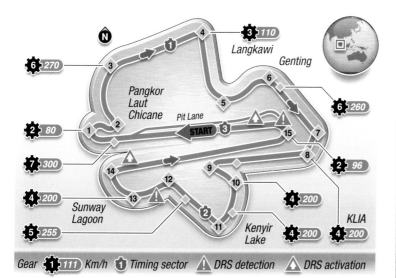

Gear ⚙ 111 Km/h ① Timing sector ⚠ DRS detection ⚠ DRS activation

2013 POLE TIME: **VETTEL (RED BULL)**, 1M49.674S, 113.048MPH/181.933KPH
2013 WINNER'S AVERAGE SPEED: 116.961MPH/188.231KPH

2013 FASTEST LAP: **PEREZ (McLAREN)**, 1M39.199S, 125.000MPH/201.168KPH
LAP RECORD: **MONTOYA (WILLIAMS)**, 1M34.223S, 131.991MPH/212.419KPH, 2004

SAKHIR

Not long ago, it would have been difficult to conceive of a grand prix being held in the Middle East, but in F1's new world order, this will be Bahrain's 10th grand prix.

The changes to the World Championship calendar have become ever more frequent in the past decade. What was once largely a season based in Europe has become global, and watching the teams racing on a circuit in a desert no longer comes as a shock. This year, though, the Bahrain race will look different as floodlights have been fitted so that it can, like neighbouring Abu Dhabi's grand prix, start later and run from daylight into darkness.

Bahrain broke new ground in 2004 when its oil revenues helped to bring a top-level international sporting event to its shores. With no history of motor sport other than holding some rally raids, there was a blank canvas for Hermann Tilke when he designed the circuit at Sakhir. He created one that bore many of his trademark features, such as a lap starting with a tight corner into a long straight into another tight corner. He then used his imagination to divide it into distinct zones, with the section around the pits and main grandstand given heavily watered grass verges to help it seem like an oasis, while the back section is desert, with sand kept from blowing across the track by a thin glue being sprayed onto the surrounding area.

The circuit's mixture of corners offers some of every type from fast to slow, with passing possible into Turn 4, but almost invariably not quite happening.

"Apart from the long lefthander in the middle of the lap which is tricky, the rest of the lap of Sakhir is straightforward and there's not much high-speed stuff." **Daniel Ricciardo**

72

INSIDE TRACK
BAHRAIN GRAND PRIX

Date:	6 April
Circuit name:	**Bahrain International Circuit**
Circuit length:	**3.363 miles/5.412km**
Number of laps:	**57**
Email:	**info@bic.com.bh**
Website:	**www.bahraingp.com.bh**

PREVIOUS WINNERS		
2004	**Michael Schumacher**	FERRARI
2005	**Fernando Alonso**	RENAULT
2006	**Fernando Alonso**	RENAULT
2007	**Felipe Massa**	FERRARI
2008	**Felipe Massa**	FERRARI
2009	**Jenson Button**	BRAWN
2010	**Fernando Alonso**	FERRARI
2012	**Sebastian Vettel**	RED BULL
2013	**Sebastian Vettel**	RED BULL

Bahrain's greatest race: A lack of overtaking has been a bugbear of the nine Bahrain GPs held to date, but the best race came in 2009 when Brawn GP driver Jenson Button had to be really gutsy to out-brake Lewis Hamilton's McLaren into Turn 1 on the second lap. That still left the Toyotas of Timo Glock and Jarno Trulli to pass, but he did, to make it three wins from the first four rounds.

Most successful Bahraini driver: The building of an international-standard circuit and hosting a grand prix for a decade has not yet led to a local driver reaching the level to race in Formula One. The most highly ranked thus far has been Hamad Al Fardan, who tried GP2 in the 2008 Asian series but has since retired. Salman Al Khalifa now competes in sportscar racing.

Best corner: The Turn 5/6/7 sequence is an excellent stretch of track, with drivers carrying as much momentum into the first part of the esse as they dare while hoping that they won't find sand blown into their path that will cost them grip.

Location: The site of the Bahrain International Circuit is a rock-strewn stretch of desert at Sakhir to the south of the capital city, Manama. A causeway from more populous Saudi Arabia to this island state helps regional fans to access the circuit.

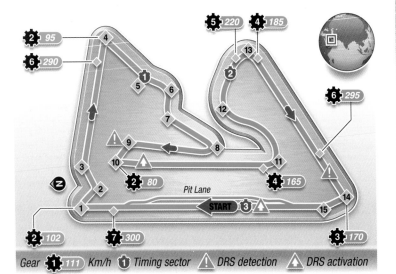

Gear ① 111 Km/h ① Timing sector ⚠ DRS detection ⚠ DRS activation

2013 POLE TIME: ROSBERG (MERCEDES), 1M32.330S, 131.125MPH/211.026KPH

2013 WINNER'S AVERAGE SPEED: 119.696MPH/192.632KPH

2013 FASTEST LAP: VETTEL (RED BULL), 1M36.961S, 124.857MPH/200.938KPH

LAP RECORD: M. SCHUMACHER (FERRARI), 1M30.252S, 134.262MPH/216.074KPH, 2004

SHANGHAI

This ultra-modern circuit remains something of an enigma. It has everything required for great racing but no atmosphere, because there are not enough fans in the grandstands.

Question: what's the difference between the Shanghai International Circuit and the Shanghai Bund, the city's main street facing onto the River Whangpoo? Answer: only the latter has any hustle and bustle. Actually, this can be something of a misconception, as the team personnel are rushing about in their usual numbers at the circuit, but this activity is diluted by the sheer scale of the paddock – it's by far the largest that the teams visit all year and people almost get lost there. In fact, everything at the circuit is built on a truly giant scale, with Formula One's tallest grandstands dwarfing the pit straight and making even a decent crowd seem to disappear. On the first two days

of a grand prix, though, few attend, and another giant grandstand at the complex of corners preceding the start of the back straight is invariably empty. Formula One still has to catch on in China, and this may well remain the case until a Chinese driver is competing at the sport's highest level.

The circuit is a good one, though, with the constantly curling first cluster of corners offering chances of passing and repassing. The esse of Turn 7 to 8 is interesting and the immensely long run down the back straight provides a good opportunity to get into position for a passing move on the way into the hairpin at Turn 14.

"It's an interesting track, particularly the first few corners that are long and tightening a lot, then the lap opens up a bit and flows in the middle sector." **Daniel Ricciardo**

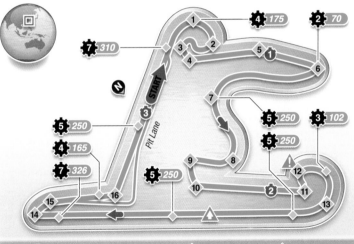

Gear 🔧 111 Km/h ① Timing sector ⚠ DRS detection ⚠ DRS activation

2013 POLE TIME: **HAMILTON (MERCEDES)**, 1M34.484S, 129.165MPH/207.871KPH
2013 WINNER'S AVERAGE SPEED: 117.929MPH/189.788KPH

2013 FASTEST LAP: **VETTEL (RED BULL)**, 1M36.808S, 125.955MPH/202.706KPH
LAP RECORD: **M. SCHUMACHER (FERRARI)**, 1M32.238S, 132.202MPH/212.759KPH, 2004

INSIDE TRACK
CHINESE GRAND PRIX

Date:	**20 April**
Circuit name:	**Shanghai International Circuit**
Circuit length:	**3.390 miles/5.450km**
Number of laps:	**56**
Email:	**f1@china-sss.com**
Website:	**www.f1china.com.cn**

PREVIOUS WINNERS

2004	**Rubens Barrichello** FERRARI
2005	**Fernando Alonso** RENAULT
2006	**Michael Schumacher** FERRARI
2007	**Kimi Raikkonen** FERRARI
2008	**Lewis Hamilton** McLAREN
2009	**Sebastian Vettel** RED BULL
2010	**Jenson Button** McLAREN
2011	**Lewis Hamilton** McLAREN
2012	**Nico Rosberg** MERCEDES
2013	**Fernando Alonso** FERRARI

F1 in China: Save for a street race in the then Portuguese enclave of Macau on the South China coast, there was no history of motor racing in China until a sportscar street race in nearby Zhuhai in 1996 was followed by the construction of the country's first permanent racing circuit there in 1998. This hoped to land a Chinese GP, but the finances weren't in place and so that went instead to Shanghai from 2004.

Most successful Chinese driver: Thus far, Ma Qing Hua is the only Chinese driver to have driven in a grand prix meeting. He did this for HRT in practice sessions in 2012, then again occasionally for Caterham last year. With testing limited, he also raced briefly in GP2 in 2013 to gain experience. Before him, Ho-Pin Tung was given a test run by Williams in 2004.

Best corner: Turn 1, as it's not just a tricky right at the end of a long straight but turns uphill and straight into Turn 2.

Location: The plot picked for the construction of this ultra-modern circuit was some boggy ground around 20 miles north of the centre of China's main financial city. Huge polystyrene blocks had to be sunk into the ground to stabilize it before building could commence.

BARCELONA

The first race of the European season offers Fernando Alonso his annual opportunity to impress at home and the teams their first chance to drive rather than fly their equipment to the venue.

The feel of the Spanish GP is markedly different to the opening races of the season as it's easier on the teams, who no longer have to pack up the minimum of equipment that they can get away with and airfreight it to the far side of the world. Races at the Circuit de Catalunya offer the first opportunity for teams to simply load whatever they want into their transporters and drive it out from their team bases. Any late development parts, of which there are many at this early stage of the season, can be flown out in just a few hours. On top of that, the teams all have their full hospitality structures for the first time, giving them space in which to go about their business and the equipment needed to do so.

The circuit itself has a decent flow down to Turn 1, up to Turn 4 then down again and back up the slope to Turn 9, Campsa, before a decent back straight down to Turn 10. The end of the lap was changed in 2007, when the insertion of a chicane perhaps reduced the chance of a chasing car catching a slipstream tow down the start/finish straight, although this doesn't matter so much now that the drivers have KERS and DRS to assist them in overtaking.

> "The straight needs good speed as it's over a kilometre long. Turn 5 needs massive downhill braking, while Turn 9 is more than 200kph, with a blind exit." **Fernando Alonso**

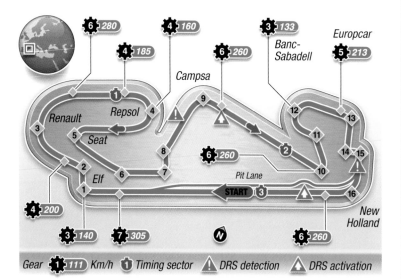

Gear 🛞1 111 Km/h ⬡1 Timing sector ⚠ DRS detection 🔺 DRS activation

2013 POLE TIME: ROSBERG (MERCEDES), 1M20.718S, 129.003MPH/207.611KPH
2013 WINNER'S AVERAGE SPEED: 115.329MPH/185.605KPH

2013 FASTEST LAP: GUTIERREZ (SAUBER), 1M26.217S, 120.776MPH/194.370KPH
LAP RECORD: RAIKKONEN (FERRARI), 1M21.670S, 127.500MPH/205.192KPH, 2008

INSIDE TRACK
SPANISH GRAND PRIX

Date:	**11 May**
Circuit name:	**Circuit de Catalunya**
Circuit length:	**2.892 miles/4.654km**
Number of laps:	**66**
Telephone:	**(34) 935 719700**
Website:	**www.circuitcat.com**

PREVIOUS WINNERS		
2004	**Michael Schumacher**	FERRARI
2005	**Kimi Raikkonen**	McLAREN
2006	**Fernando Alonso**	RENAULT
2007	**Felipe Massa**	FERRARI
2008	**Kimi Raikkonen**	FERRARI
2009	**Jenson Button**	BRAWN
2010	**Mark Webber**	RED BULL
2011	**Sebastian Vettel**	RED BULL
2012	**Pastor Maldonado**	WILLIAMS
2013	**Fernando Alonso**	FERRARI

F1 in Spain: The grand prix has moved around Spain a fair bit. Barcelona has hosted grands prix at three different venues, with Pedralbes and Montjuich Park preceding this one. The race then moved to Jarama outside Madrid and later to Jerez in the south-west.

Most successful Spanish driver: Double World Champion Fernando Alonso is by far the most successful driver for Spain. Indeed, he's the only winner, and only two others have even stepped onto an F1 podium. These were Alfonso de Portago, second for Ferrari at Silverstone in 1956, and Pedro de la Rosa, second for McLaren in Hungary in 2006.

Best corner: Turn 9, Campsa, remains the best challenge for the drivers, as they have to hit the apex as they crest the rise and anyone running wide will lose precious momentum onto the back straight. However, Turn 1, Elf, is the best corner as this righthander with a downhill approach is the only point on the lap where overtaking is likely.

Location: The Circuit de Catalunya is located on a gentle hillside out beyond the northern suburbs of Barcelona, 12 miles from the city centre, and can be reached easily by car up the A17 motorway. It is also possible to get there from the city by train to Montmelo station, then walking the last bit.

MONACO

F1 really wouldn't be F1 without Monaco; despite being an unsuitable place for cars of such prodigious performance to race, it offers the glitz and glamour that the sport needs.

Only a cluster of circuits on the 2014 Formula One calendar have much history to them. Some have been hosting grands prix for quarter of a century and more, but Monaco stands with Silverstone, Monza and Spa-Francorchamps in having been around since the World Championship began in 1950. You don't have to think hard to conjure images of some fabulous action and incident on its narrow streets over the intervening decades.

Yet, while the other three of this group offer high-speed racing, Monaco is quite the opposite; it's in the middle of a town, for starters, hemmed in between the harbour and a steep hillside covered in buildings. There is precious little space for the cars to

fly as they rise up to Casino Square, plunge down to Portier, then blast through the tunnel and snake around the swimming pool, but the setting is magical, every camera angle affording an interesting backdrop.

For the drivers, every lap carries risk, as the barriers are all-enclosing and a slight slip can spell disaster. Yet they all know that a win here carries more prestige than any other all year. Monaco is perhaps doubly important to their sponsors, watching from their yachts, and strong performances here by their team's cars go a long way to securing the ever essential reinvestment for the following year, thus helping the F1 teams to keep their wheels turning.

> "It's great to race in the city where I live and I love being able to ride into the paddock from home on a scooter." **Nico Rosberg**

INSIDE TRACK
MONACO GRAND PRIX

Date:	**25 May**
Circuit name:	**Monte Carlo Circuit**
Circuit length:	**2.075 miles/3.339km**
Number of laps:	**78**
Email:	**info@acm.mc**
Website:	**www.acm.mc**

PREVIOUS WINNERS

2004	**Jarno Trulli** RENAULT
2005	**Kimi Raikkonen** McLAREN
2006	**Fernando Alonso** RENAULT
2007	**Fernando Alonso** McLAREN
2008	**Lewis Hamilton** McLAREN
2009	**Jenson Button** BRAWN
2010	**Mark Webber** RED BULL
2011	**Sebastian Vettel** RED BULL
2012	**Mark Webber** RED BULL
2013	**Nico Rosberg** MERCEDES

F1 in Monaco: The principality's first grand prix was in 1929, so it was well and truly established as a racing venue when the World Championship started in 1950 and has held a grand prix every year since bar 1951, when there was no event, and 1952, when it was held for sportscars.

Most successful Monegasque driver: Although most F1 drivers base themselves in Monaco for tax reasons, only a few have hailed from there. Louis Chiron drove a works Maserati to third on home ground in 1950. Later, Olivier Beretta had a season with Larrousse in 1994. Greatest success has been achieved by second-generation racers Jacques Villeneuve and Nico Rosberg, who were brought up there.

Best corner: Massenet offers the biggest challenge as drivers attempt to carry as much speed as possible through this hilltop lefthander into Casino Square.

Location: The circuit is in the heart of Monte Carlo, with its lap using the streets at the foot of the hill beneath the Grimaldis' castle, then scaling the rise on the other side of the harbour towards Casino Square, then down the other side to meet the seafront road towards Menton before doubling back along the harbour front.

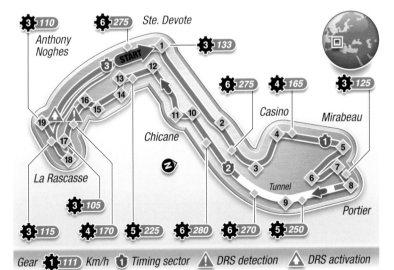

Ste. Devote — *Anthony Noghes* — START — *Chicane* — *Casino* — *Mirabeau* — *La Rascasse* — *Tunnel* — *Portier*

Gear | 1 | 111 | Km/h | 1 | Timing sector | ⚠ DRS detection | ⚠ DRS activation

2013 POLE TIME: **ROSBERG (MERCEDES),** 1M13.876S, 101.134MPH/162.759KPH
2013 WINNER'S AVERAGE SPEED: **70.450MPH/113.378KPH**

2013 FASTEST LAP: **VETTEL (RED BULL),** 1M16.577S, 97.566MPH/157.018KPH
LAP RECORD: **RAIKKONEN (FERRARI),** 1M21.670S, 127.500MPH/205.192KPH, 2008

Fernando Alonso lets rip with the champagne after taking his second win of the year for Ferrari, this one at his home track outside Barcelona.

MONTREAL

This circuit is hard on the cars and not at all relaxing for the drivers as it twists around its island setting, but it remains one of the most popular on the calendar as everyone loves the city.

If the circuit at Monaco is hemmed in by the buildings, then Montreal's Circuit Gilles Villeneuve is hemmed in by water. Built on a long, thin island in the St Lawrence River, it makes the most of the narrow plot, even feeding itself between an ornamental lake on one side and Montreal's Olympic rowing lake.

The lap's opening sequence of three corners, a slight right kink followed by a tight left then an even tighter right, causes problems annually as the cars arrive there on the first lap. However, the field is then forced to run one behind the other through the series of five twisting corners around the back of the circuit before drivers might consider a passing bid into the hairpin known as l'Epingle. From here, it's a long blast back towards the pits, with a right/left flick of a chicane often completing the lap with explosive action. If incident alone doesn't reduce the field of cars, then the long periods running at full throttle and the heavy braking into the tight corners can.

While the United States of America has spent decades trying to find a venue that becomes a regular and well-attended home for its grand prix, this very popular circuit has been a mainstay, providing spectacular racing and so keeping Formula One in the public eye in North America.

"It's the shortest lap of the season and it's a great track with big braking and if you don't touch the kerbs at the chicane it's good. The city is always fun too." **Charles Pic**

INSIDE TRACK
CANADIAN GRAND PRIX

Date:	**8 June**
Circuit name:	**Circuit Gilles Villeneuve**
Circuit length:	**2.710 miles/4.361km**
Number of laps:	**70**
Email:	**info@circuitgillesvilleneuve.ca**
Website:	**www.circuitgillesvilleneuve.ca**

PREVIOUS WINNERS

2003	**Michael Schumacher** FERRARI
2004	**Michael Schumacher** FERRARI
2005	**Kimi Raikkonen** McLAREN
2006	**Fernando Alonso** RENAULT
2007	**Lewis Hamilton** McLAREN
2008	**Robert Kubica** BMW SAUBER
2010	**Lewis Hamilton** McLAREN
2011	**Jenson Button** McLAREN
2012	**Lewis Hamilton** McLAREN
2013	**Sebastian Vettel** RED BULL

F1 in Canada: Canada's grand prix was held for sportscars until 1967, when Mosport Park landed a round of the World Championship. Apart from two grands prix held at Quebec's St Jovite, the race stayed there until 1977. The event was then revamped by being moved to Montreal, where Gilles Villeneuve gave the venue its dream launch by winning.

Most successful Canadian driver: Gilles Villeneuve was the first Canadian driver to make his mark in Formula One, finishing as runner-up to his Ferrari team-mate Jody Scheckter in 1979. However, after his death in 1982, it was his son Jacques who became the country's only World Champion thus far, with Williams in 1997.

Best corner: The chicane that completes the lap is where the action is, as drivers attempt to complete a passing move and still get their braking done to slow enough to flick right then left.

Location: The Ile de Notre Dame on which the circuit is built is an island near the southern bank of the St Lawrence Seaway in the eastern end of the city. The island was first known for hosting the international EXPO trade fair in 1967 and later for being the home of the rowing lake used when Montreal hosted the 1976 Olympic Games.

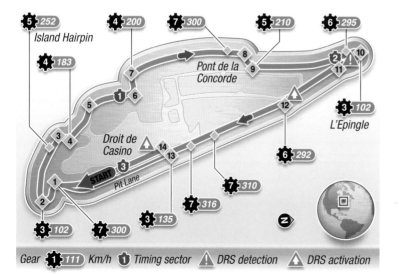

Gear ① 111 Km/h ① Timing sector ⚠ DRS detection ⚠ DRS activation

2013 POLE TIME: VETTEL (RED BULL), 1M25.425S, 114.197MPH/183.782KPH
2013 WINNER'S AVERAGE SPEED: 123.503MPH/198.759KPH

2013 FASTEST LAP: WEBBER (RED BULL), 1M16.182S, 128.052MPH/206.080KPH
LAP RECORD: BARRICHELLO (FERRARI), 1M13.622S, 132.511MPH/213.256KPH, 2004

RED BULL RING

This circuit is now in its third incarnation. It started life as the Osterreichring, was shortened to become the A1-Ring and has now been revived and rebranded by the energy drink company.

When the A1-Ring hosted the Austrian GP for the last time in 2003, it seemed that the country of World Champions Jochen Rindt and Niki Lauda had held its final grand prix, with wealthier countries in the Far East lining up to take its place on the increasingly over-subscribed calendar. Yet now, a decade on, it's back.

The venue overlooking the valley floor Zeltweg airfield that hosted the Austrian GP in 1964 remains spectacular, its plot ensuring that the track has gradient changes like few others; and the flow of the lap is as before, starting with a steep climb to the first corner, then a more gentle rise all the way up to the tight right over a crest at Turn 2, Remus. The circuit then crosses the face of the hillside before twisting its way back down again to the old Niki Lauda Kurve, then running across the hill again behind the paddock, before feeding through a pair of righthanders back onto the start/finish straight. There had been talk of major redevelopment work in 2004 when Red Bull magnate Dietrich Mateschitz bought it, and the pit buildings and main grandstand were demolished, but the track has been kept as before.

Weather can be changeable here, but the event's June date means the race ought to escape the midsummer heat that can give way to thunderstorms.

> "The time when Formula One raced here last is not that long ago, so it will be nice to see F1 coming back." **Sebastian Vettel**

INSIDE TRACK
AUSTRIAN GRAND PRIX

Date:	**22 June**
Circuit name:	**Red Bull Ring**
Circuit length:	**2.688 miles/4.326km**
Number of laps:	**71**
Email: information@projekt-spielberg.at	
Website:	**www.projekt-spielberg.at**

PREVIOUS WINNERS		
1985	**Alain Prost**	McLAREN
1986	**Alain Prost**	McLAREN
1987	**Nigel Mansell**	WILLIAMS
1997	**Jacques Villeneuve**	WILLIAMS
1998	**Mika Hakkinen**	McLAREN
1999	**Eddie Irvine**	FERRARI
2000	**Mika Hakkinen**	McLAREN
2001	**David Coulthard**	McLAREN
2002	**Michael Schumacher**	FERRARI
2003	**Michael Schumacher**	FERRARI

F1 in Austria: Formula One's first foray to Austria was for a non-championship race on the Zeltweg airfield circuit in 1963. This was followed by a World Championship round there the following year, but the circuit was thought too bumpy. Austria didn't host another grand prix until 1970, when it moved up the hill to the Osterreichring, where it stayed until 1987. Considered too fast and thus not safe, this was modified and cut in length to return as the A1-Ring in 1997, but this was dropped after 2003.

Most successful Austrian driver: Austria is a country that has punched above its weight. Although Jochen Rindt didn't live to see his crowning as World Champion in 1970, Niki Lauda was fortunate to survive a fiery accident in 1976 and went on to claim his third F1 title in 1984.

Best corner: The Jochen Rindt Kurve, the last corner but one, is the trickiest as drivers have to keep as much speed as they dare through the dipping exit.

Location: The circuit is far from any area of notable population, with Graz the closest city, and that's 45 miles to the south-east. Vienna and Salzburg are both around 125 miles away, to the north-east and north-west respectively.

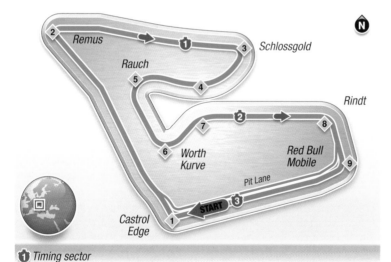

🏁 Timing sector

2003 POLE TIME: **BARRICHELLO (FERRARI)**, 1M08.082S, 142.137MPH/228.747KPH

2003 WINNER'S AVERAGE SPEED: **132.354MPH/213.003KPH**

2003 FASTEST LAP: **M SCHUMACHER (FERRARI)**, 1M08.337S, 141.606MPH/227.894KPH

LAP RECORD: **M SCHUMACHER (FERRARI)**, 1M08.337S, 141.606MPH/227.894KPH, 2003

SILVERSTONE

When the sun shines and the grandstands and spectator banking are packed, this is one of the world's greatest motor racing venues, to say nothing of its lengthy sporting pedigree.

Silverstone is both ancient and modern. It's ancient as racing has been held here since someone thought of a better use for a World War II airfield in 1948, and modern, like a garden fork with a new handle, having been changed constantly across the intervening decades. While the layout has been realigned and the facilities kept contemporary, the very nature of the place has remained the same. It's a high-speed circuit that offers the drivers a true challenge.

The lap used to start before Copse, but since 2010 it has started between Club and Abbey, in front of the huge new pits complex known as The Wing. The early corners of the lap are wide enough for drivers to jostle side by side, with a good tow down the Wellington Straight helping some to overtake into Brooklands. What really excites the drivers, though, is the Becketts complex, a right/left/right sequence of sweepers taken at over 150mph. A good exit from the last part of these, Chapel, can then help a driver to catch a tow down Hangar Straight towards Stowe, with a final passing opportunity coming after that if a driver can dive up the inside at the end of the Vale.

Rain can spice up the action and the stoic fans are certainly not going to quit their vantage points should it fall.

"It's a really spectacular venue with some of the greatest corners of the year and the atmosphere is incredible, with the place packed all weekend." **Paul di Resta**

80

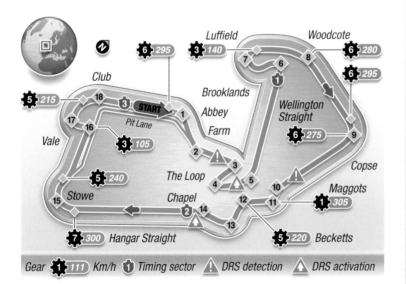

Gear ⚙1️⃣ 111 Km/h 1️⃣ Timing sector ⚠ DRS detection ⚠ DRS activation

2013 POLE TIME: **ROSBERG (MERCEDES)**, 1M29.607S, 147.062MPH/236.673KPH
2013 WINNER'S AVERAGE SPEED: 122.762MPH/197.566KPH

2013 FASTEST LAP: **WEBBER (RED BULL)**, 1M33.401S, 141.088MPH/227.059KPH
LAP RECORD: **ALONSO (FERRARI)**, 1M30.874S, 145.011MPH/233.373KPH, 2011

INSIDE TRACK
BRITISH GRAND PRIX

Date:	6 July
Circuit name:	Silverstone
Circuit length:	3.659 miles/5.900km
Number of laps:	52
Email:	sales@silverstone-circuit.co.uk
Website:	www.silverstone-circuit.co.uk

PREVIOUS WINNERS

2004	**Michael Schumacher** FERRARI
2005	**Juan Pablo Montoya** McLAREN
2006	**Fernando Alonso** RENAULT
2007	**Kimi Raikkonen** FERRARI
2008	**Lewis Hamilton** McLAREN
2009	**Sebastian Vettel** RED BULL
2010	**Mark Webber** RED BULL
2011	**Fernando Alonso** FERRARI
2012	**Mark Webber** RED BULL
2013	**Nico Rosberg** MERCEDES

F1 in Great Britain: The British have always loved motor racing, and that passion was fired by the 1907 opening of Brooklands, Europe's first purpose-built circuit. Silverstone took over after World War II, hosting the first ever World Championship round in 1950. Since then, Aintree and Brands Hatch have both also hosted the British GP, and Donington Park was allocated the European GP slot in 1993.

Most successful British driver: Jackie Stewart is the only British driver to have collected three F1 titles, with Jim Clark and Graham Hill having taken two apiece. Stewart was first crowned when racing a Matra in 1969, then again with Tyrrell in 1971 and 1973.

Best corner: Becketts is not just the best at Silverstone but one of the best in the world, as this sixth-gear right/left/right sequence is ferociously fast and the rapid changes of direction are almost beyond the belief of the spectators there.

Location: Silverstone has drawn in huge crowds over the years, its central location 15 miles west of Northampton in England's Midlands putting it in a couple of hours' reach of the majority of the population. The flat site to the west of Towcester was formerly an airfield.

HOCKENHEIM

Still alternating with the Nurburgring, it's Hockenheim's turn to host the German GP this year, offering the drivers a different challenge as Sebastian Vettel goes for gold again.

It seems inconceivable, bearing in mind Germany's strong involvement in the motor industry, and all the titles and wins gathered by Michael Schumacher then Sebastian Vettel, that the country's grand prix is increasingly in the balance. Yet, when the 2014 calendar was being discussed, there was even talk that the event might alternate not just between Hockenheim and the Nurburgring but between Germany and Austria now that the Red Bull Ring is back in business.

For this year at least, the German GP remains, and this circuit in the forests to the south of Heidelberg will ring to the sound of Formula One engines once more.

Since its emasculation in 2002 when it lost most of its long loop through the forest, the track has been a shadow of its former self, losing its characteristic long blasts interrupted only by chicanes. Now it has just one long arcing stretch, from Turn 4 to Turn 6, Spitzkehre, allowing the drivers not only to stretch their legs but to line up the car ahead for a possible passing move into the righthand hairpin. The stadium section from Turn 12, Mobil 1, to the exit of the first corner remains as it has been for decades, with huge grandstands packed with flag-waving fans. When you see this, you wonder how the circuit is struggling to keep up financially, as all looks well.

"I won here often in my early career and will never forget my father's last DTM race here in 1995 as I joined him on the roof of his car through the stadium section." **Nico Rosberg**

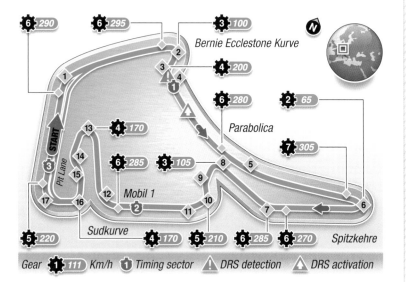

Bernie Ecclestone Kurve

Parabolica

Mobil 1

Sudkurve

Spitzkehre

Gear ● 111 Km/h ● Timing sector ⚠ DRS detection ⚠ DRS activation

---

2012 POLE TIME: **ALONSO (FERRARI)**, 1M40.621S, 101.685MPH/163.647KPH
2012 WINNER'S AVERAGE SPEED: **125.419MPH/201.843KPH**

2012 FASTEST LAP: **M SCHUMACHER (MERCEDES)**, 1M18.725S, 129.968MPH/209.163KPH
LAP RECORD: **RAIKKONEN (McLAREN)**, 1M14.917S, 136.567MPH/219.784KPH, 2004

INSIDE TRACK
GERMAN GRAND PRIX

Date:	**20 July**
Circuit name:	**Hockenheim**
Circuit length:	**2.842 miles/4.574km**
Number of laps:	**67**
Email:	**Info@hockenheimring.de**
Website:	**www.hockenheimring.de**

PREVIOUS WINNERS

2000	**Rubens Barrichello** FERRARI
2001	**Ralf Schumacher** WILLIAMS
2002	**Michael Schumacher** FERRARI
2003	**Juan Pablo Montoya** WILLIAMS
2004	**Michael Schumacher** FERRARI
2005	**Fernando Alonso** RENAULT
2006	**Michael Schumacher** FERRARI
2008	**Lewis Hamilton** McLAREN
2010	**Fernando Alonso** FERRARI
2012	**Fernando Alonso** FERRARI

F1 in Germany: Germany didn't host a round of the inaugural World Championship, but a race at the Nurburgring was included in 1951 and its 14-mile Nordschleife layout was used until 1976 when Niki Lauda suffered terrible burns. The partially banked AVUS circuit in Berlin had been used in 1959 and Hockenheim in 1970, and it was to the latter that the grand prix returned in 1977. It has been held there ever since, alternating with the Nurburgring since 2007.

Most successful German driver: For all the excellence of Mercedes-Benz in the mid-1950s, Germany failed to have a World Champion until Michael Schumacher won his first title in 1994. Wolfgang von Trips was tipped to win in 1961 but was killed at Monza, and it wasn't until Jochen Mass won in Spain in 1975 that another German driver won a grand prix. Schumacher and Sebastian Vettel have now won 11 titles between them.

Best corner: There's only one surefire spot to watch overtaking at Hockenheim, and this is at Spitzkehre, at the end of the back straight. It's tight in and tight out.

Location: Tucked into a forest on flat land 15 miles south of Heidelberg, Hockenheim draws much of its crowd from Frankfurt and Stuttgart 55 and 85 miles away respectively.

HUNGARORING

When this race was introduced it was seen as one that wouldn't stay long on the calendar, but the Hungaroring has been hosting a grand prix for 27 years and shows no sign of dropping out.

Hungary was still a communist country when Formula One ringmaster Bernie Ecclestone did a deal to go behind the Iron Curtain and hold a grand prix there in 1986. The contrasts with this most capitalist of sports were extraordinary but the fans turned out in their tens of thousands. It was a sell-out and the race has enticed increasing numbers of fans from other countries in the intervening years, a notable ingredient of the make-up being the Finns cheering for first Mika Hakkinen and then more recently Kimi Raikkonen, as it's their closest grand prix. Until his injury in 2011, Robert Kubica ensured the Polish fans had someone to cheer on too.

On paper, the circuit looks great, snaking its way down, across and up a valley before traversing the opposite bank and then diving back into the valley for the homeward leg. The topography offers fans incredible views of the racing. Sadly, so twisting are the corners that there is precious little scope for them to allow much overtaking action. Indeed, barring heroic moves into Turn 1 and perhaps Turn 2 on the opening lap, most changes of order happen in the pits.

The climate can be uncomfortably hot and humid around the time of its high summer date, but the fans and team personnel enjoy cooling down in Budapest in the evenings.

> "I love the layout of the circuit and Budapest is a really cool city which has a great atmosphere over the race weekend."
> **Lewis Hamilton**

82

INSIDE TRACK
HUNGARIAN GRAND PRIX

Date:	**27 July**
Circuit name:	**Hungaroring**
Circuit length:	**2.722 miles/4.381km**
Number of laps:	**70**
Email:	**office@hungaroring.hu**
Website:	**www.hungaroring.hu**

PREVIOUS WINNERS

2004	**Michael Schumacher** FERRARI
2005	**Kimi Raikkonen** McLAREN
2006	**Jenson Button** HONDA
2007	**Lewis Hamilton** McLAREN
2008	**Heikki Kovalainen** McLAREN
2009	**Lewis Hamilton** McLAREN
2010	**Mark Webber** RED BULL
2011	**Jenson Button** McLAREN
2012	**Lewis Hamilton** McLAREN
2013	**Lewis Hamilton** MERCEDES

F1 in Hungary: Hungary hosted a grand prix as long ago as 1936, when Tazio Nuvolari won for Alfa Romeo in Budapest's Nepliget Park. After that, it took half a century for a round of the World Championship to be granted to Hungary, but the circuit has defied expectations by remaining on the calendar ever since.

Most successful Hungarian driver: Only one Hungarian driver has competed in the World Championship since its inception in 1950. That was Zsolt Baumgartner, who turned out for Jordan in 2003 and Minardi in 2004. However, Hungary can proudly claim that one of its own won the first ever grand prix, the French GP in 1906. This was Ferenc Szisz at the wheel of a Renault.

Best corner: High-speed corners are few and far between at the Hungaroring, so Turn 4 stands out. It's little more than a lefthand kink taken as the cars climb from the bottom of the valley, but it's made more critical as drivers can't see over the brow and yet immediately have to place themselves in preparation for the slower Turn 5.

Location: Built in rolling countryside at Mogyrod, north-east of Budapest, the Hungaroring is just 12 miles away from the capital's centre.

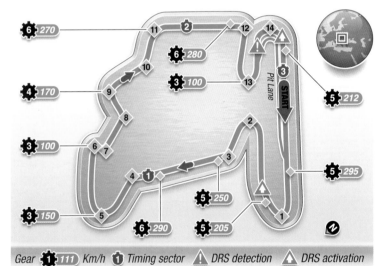

Gear **1** 111 Km/h **1** Timing sector ⚠ DRS detection ⚠ DRS activation

2013 POLE TIME: HAMILTON (MERCEDES), 1M19.388S, 123.444MPH/198.664KPH
2013 WINNER'S AVERAGE SPEED: 111.540MPH/179.506KPH

2013 FASTEST LAP: WEBBER (RED BULL), 1M24.069S, 116.571MPH/187.603KPH
LAP RECORD: M SCHUMACHER (FERRARI), 1M19.071S, 123.828MPH/199.282KPH, 2004

SPA-FRANCORCHAMPS

It tends to rain here, a lot, but nothing can take away from the magical atmosphere of this very special circuit as it rises and falls, with some seriously quick corners to entertain spectators.

For many long-time fans of motor racing, Spa-Francorchamps is the very template of how a great circuit should be as it offers some extremely testing high-speed corners, uses the slopes of its hillside setting to incredible effect and mixes racing with the beauty of Mother Nature as it threads its way through the Ardennes forest. It also drips with history, having been open for racing since 1924. It could thus not be more different to some of the circuits that have been welcomed into the World Championship across the past decade. This is the real thing.

The lap starts innocuously enough, with a short dash up a gentle slope to the La Source hairpin. Then it doubles back, drops down the hill to Eau Rouge, where drivers flick left, right, left and up over the brow at Raidillon. The straight that follows offers the chance of a tow and thus possible passing into Les Combes. The downhill twists after that are tricky, before the ascent from Paul Frere via Blanchimont to the Bus Stop, requiring fortitude.

If this isn't testing enough, rain is no stranger to the region and makes matters even more difficult by sometimes falling only on one end of the circuit. So, mix all these factors together and you can understand why a win here is worth two wins anywhere else.

"Spa is a different challenge with an incredibly long lap and fantastic mix of long straights and high-speed corners. It's definitely one of my favourites." **Max Chilton**

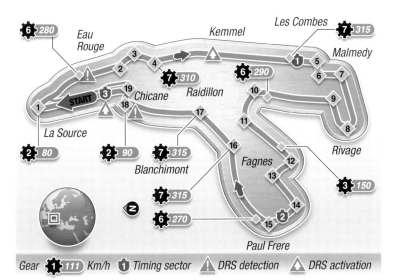

Eau Rouge
Kemmel
Les Combes
Malmedy
Raidillon
START
La Source
Chicane
Blanchimont
Fagnes
Rivage
Paul Frere

Gear ⚙ 111 Km/h · 1 Timing sector · ⚠ DRS detection · ⚠ DRS activation

2013 POLE TIME: **HAMILTON (MERCEDES)**, 2M01.012S, 129.470MPH/208.362KPH
2013 WINNER'S AVERAGE SPEED: 137.209MPH/220.817KPH

2013 FASTEST LAP: **VETTEL (RED BULL)**, 1M50.756S, 141.459MPH/227.657KPH
LAP RECORD: **VETTEL (RED BULL)**, 1M47.263S, 146.065MPH/235.069KPH, 2009

INSIDE TRACK
BELGIAN GRAND PRIX

Date:	**24 August**
Circuit name:	**Spa-Francorchamps**
Circuit length:	**4.352 miles/7.004km**
Number of laps:	**44**
Email: **secretariat@spa-francorchamps.be**	
Website: **www.spa-francorchamps.be**	

PREVIOUS WINNERS	
2002	**Michael Schumacher** FERRARI
2004	**Kimi Raikkonen** McLAREN
2005	**Kimi Raikkonen** McLAREN
2007	**Kimi Raikkonen** FERRARI
2008	**Felipe Massa** FERRARI
2009	**Kimi Raikkonen** FERRARI
2010	**Lewis Hamilton** McLAREN
2011	**Sebastian Vettel** RED BULL
2012	**Jenson Button** McLAREN
2013	**Sebastian Vettel** RED BULL

F1 in Belgium: Three circuits have hosted the Belgian GP. Spa-Francorchamps was the first, in 1925, and it continued until 1970, after which it was deemed too fast and so unsafe. Nivelles near capital Brussels was given the race in 1972 and 1974, it was then held at Zolder until 1984, after which the truncated Spa-Francorchamps, without the stretch through the next valley, became its home again.

Most successful Belgian driver: Jacky Ickx tops the table, having won eight grands prix between 1968 and 1972 and been runner-up in the World Championship in 1970. Thierry Boutsen is the next most successful, with three wins and a best ranking of fourth for Benetton in 1988.

Best corner: Now that Eau Rouge holds no fear for the drivers, Pouhon is the king of the circuit's corners. This downhill double lefthander is a tricky but vital part of the circuit's flow on the descent from the Rivage hairpin to its lowest point, Paul Frere.

Location: The forested setting that is draped with the Spa-Francorchamps circuit is just south of the village of Francorchamps which is, in turn, 10 miles south of the resort town of Spa. The closest city is Liege, 30 miles to the north-west, with Maastricht a similar distance to the north.

The concentration on the Ferrari pit crew's faces is clear as Felipe Massa arrives for a pitstop during the season-opening Australian GP.

MONZA

Not one of the long-standing Formula One venues has changed its form over the years as little as Monza, and that is why Italy's historic circuit remains a gem with a clear link to its past.

Had it not been for the insertion of a trio of chicanes in 1972, the layout of this circuit in a royal park to the north of Milan would scarcely have changed since 1948. The chicanes were built in the name of safety, in order to slow the cars and to stop them hunting in giant, slipstreaming packs. The first chicane was inserted halfway between the start line and the first corner, the second midway through the old Roggia sweep and the last one at the open Vialone lefthander onto the back straight. They are still in use, only lightly modified, today.

The first chicane is often the scene of collisions on the opening lap, and a driver who makes a poor exit from the second part of the chicane can end up slow through Curva Grande and thus vulnerable to attack into the second chicane. The pair of Lesmos that follow are not the challenge they once were, but the final corner, Parabolica, still offers the potential for a driver to run out of road and end up in the gravel trap. So, this classic circuit keeps the drivers on their toes.

An extra element of Monza's rich history lurks among the trees on its flanks, as parts of the original banked circuit that used sometimes to be combined with the grand prix circuit can still be seen there, gradually crumbling away.

INSIDE TRACK
ITALIAN GRAND PRIX

Date:	**7 September**
Circuit name:	**Monza Circuit**
Circuit length:	**3.600 miles/5.793km**
Number of laps:	**53**
Email:	**infoautodromo@monzanet.it**
Website:	**www.monzanet.it**

PREVIOUS WINNERS

2004	**Rubens Barrichello** FERRARI
2005	**Juan Pablo Montoya** McLAREN
2006	**Michael Schumacher** FERRARI
2007	**Fernando Alonso** McLAREN
2008	**Sebastian Vettel** TORO ROSSO
2009	**Rubens Barrichello** BRAWN
2010	**Fernando Alonso** FERRARI
2011	**Sebastian Vettel** RED BULL
2012	**Lewis Hamilton** McLAREN
2013	**Sebastian Vettel** RED BULL

F1 in Italy: Italian fans are passionate about Formula One, or more especially about Ferrari, and they have had a grand prix since one was held in Brescia in 1921. Monza first hosted one in 1922 and the event has been ever present since, with the country being granted a second race each year between 1981, when Imola's race was given the courtesy title of the San Marino GP, and 2006.

Most successful Italian driver: Despite Italy being the country of Ferrari, its drivers have made nowhere near the level of impact that they should and, amazingly, there has not been an Italian World Champion since Alberto Ascari in 1953.

Best corner: The Curva Parabolica is the pick of the track, with the drivers arriving in seventh gear and trying to hold on to as much speed as they can to take onto the start/finish straight, but often running just a little wide and going for a rodeo ride, as Lewis Hamilton did in qualifying last year.

Location: Found just outside the town of Monza, which is around 10 miles north-west of Milan, the circuit is compressed into the northern side of a royal park in a wooded area that has grown up since the circuit opened in 1922.

> "I've won at Monza both in Formula Renault 3.5 and GP2 and it's the quickest track of the year, one where we run very low downforce settings." **Giedo van der Garde**

86

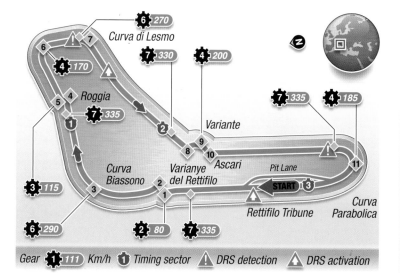

Gear ① 111 *Km/h* ① *Timing sector* ⚠ *DRS detection* ⚠ *DRS activation*

2013 POLE TIME: VETTEL (RED BULL), 1M23.755S, 154.719MPH/248.997KPH
2013 WINNER'S AVERAGE SPEED: 145.567MPH/234.268KPH

2013 FASTEST LAP: HAMILTON (RED BULL), 1M25.849S, 150.946MPH/242.924KPH
LAP RECORD: BARRICHELLO (FERRARI), 1M21.046S, 159.909MPH/257.349KPH, 2004

MARINA BAY

This venue in Singapore took Formula One into new territory – a race in a city centre in Asia, staged after nightfall. It offers a spectacle with a real difference, and is fast becoming a favourite.

When Formula One impresario Bernie Ecclestone looked to expand Formula One beyond its European heartland, this was not necessarily the sort of race that he craved, but it certainly became so once he had established new grands prix in Malaysia and China.

Holding a grand prix in the heart of a city, and a leading financial centre at that, was a definite step forward. Getting the organizers to agree to hold it after nightfall made it better still, as it looks fantastic on TV, something really different, with the city's illuminated skyline definitely one of the World Championship's most spectacular backdrops. A further advantage of its timing was that it fitted in just perfectly for an afternoon slot for the core viewing market of European fans.

Singapore is a very "can do" sort of place, and its track layout shows that it didn't let anything stand in its way as it created that rare thing, a street circuit with several decently fast stretches, most especially the one from Turn 5 to Turn 7. For all that, overtaking is still less than easy, with the entries to Turn 14 and Turn 1 the other likely options. With concrete walls lining the route, any slip-up tends to be punished. What is weird for the teams is that they don't need to be at the track until afternoon Singapore time.

"Singapore is a great place. I love the local food and don't mind the unusual times we run in the car as it means that I don't have to get up early." **Kimi Raikkonen**

INSIDE TRACK
SINGAPORE GRAND PRIX

Date:	**21 September**
Circuit name:	**Marina Bay Circuit**
Circuit length:	**3.152 miles/5.073km**
Number of laps:	**61**
Email:	**info@singaporegp.sg**
Website:	**www.singaporegp.sg**

PREVIOUS WINNERS

2008	**Fernando Alonso** RENAULT
2009	**Lewis Hamilton** McLAREN
2010	**Fernando Alonso** FERRARI
2011	**Sebastian Vettel** RED BULL
2012	**Sebastian Vettel** RED BULL
2013	**Sebastian Vettel** RED BULL

F1 in Singapore: Expatriates based in Singapore created a circuit along Thompson Road in the 1960s, but it was only in 2008 that a proper temporary facility was built, once the country had agreed to host a night race so that it could join the World Championship.

Singapore's greatest race: If a race is judged by the closeness of its finish, then the 2010 Singapore GP was the best, as Ferrari's Fernando Alonso beat Red Bull Racing's Sebastian Vettel by just 0.293s.

Most successful Singaporean driver: Dennis Lian aimed to be the country's first motor racing star in the mid-2000s but didn't progress past Formula V6 Asia or A1GP.

Best corner: Turn 1 can be the scene of explosive action on the opening lap. It's a sharp lefthander that feeds directly into a kinked right which in turn feeds into a lefthand hairpin. Being in position for one of these doesn't mean that a driver will be on the right line for the next, so it's tricky in traffic.

Location: Street races have been rare across the history of the World Championship, with Monaco the only constant. Their attraction is that they take the racing to the people and Singapore's street circuit very much does that, running around the city's central business district, circumnavigating the parks by the Raffles Hotel, crossing both the iconic Anderson Bridge and the more modern Esplanade Bridge and then running along the waterfront.

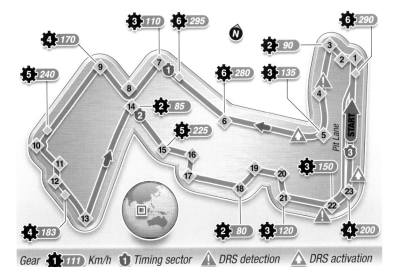

Gear **1** 111 Km/h **1** Timing sector ⚠ DRS detection ⚠ DRS activation

2013 POLE TIME: **VETTEL (RED BULL)**, 1M42.841S, 110.170MPH/177.302KPH
2013 WINNER'S AVERAGE SPEED: **96.576MPH/155.425KPH**

2013 FASTEST LAP: **VETTEL (RED BULL)**, 1M48.574S, 104.353MPH/167.940KPH
LAP RECORD: **RAIKKONEN (FERRARI)**, 1M45.599S, 107.358MPH/172.776KPH, 2008

SUZUKA

This is a circuit that has it all, with an intensely challenging strip of tarmac that dips and twists its way over a hillside then back again and challenges the drivers at almost every turn.

Suzuka is very much an old school sort of place. The compact strip of land on which it was built in 1962 wouldn't have been considered had it been offered in the past 15 years, during which Hermann Tilke has been commissioned to design Formula One's new venues. It's simply too small, without enough space for the standard paddock and other ancillaries that F1 now demands. Yet, the shape that Zandvoort designer John Hugenholtz created for Honda is what gives the place its character, with everything feeling slightly enclosed. It means the drivers can seldom relax as, save for accelerating down the start/finish straight or out of Spoon Curve onto

the back straight, they are almost always straight into the next corner. This is an extremely challenging circuit, especially through the uphill esses after the first two turns. Then 130R on the homeward leg still commands respect and the final chicane always catches out a few, especially if it rains, which it often does.

The Japanese GP has been slipping ever further forward on the World Championship calendar, and this is a shame as it used to be either the last or the penultimate race and it's very much the sort of circuit that deserves to be there to sort the great from the good in the final reckoning of a World Championship decider.

"Suzuka's esses are one of the best stretches of track we race on all year, as they're fast corners, left, right, left, really quick, floating corners." **Sebastian Vettel**

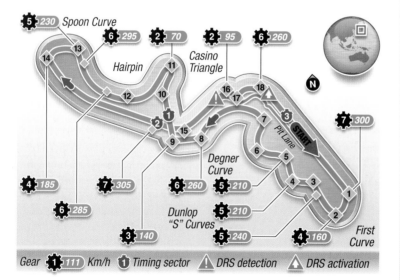

Spoon Curve · Hairpin · Casino Triangle · Degner Curve · Dunlop "S" Curves · First Curve · Pit Lane · START

Gear | Km/h | Timing sector | DRS detection | DRS activation

2013 POLE TIME: WEBBER (RED BULL), 1M30.915S, 142.879MPH/229.942KPH
2013 WINNER'S AVERAGE SPEED: 132.031MPH/212.484KPH

2013 FASTEST LAP: WEBBER (RED BULL), 1M34.587S, 137.332MPH/221.015KPH
LAP RECORD: RAIKKONEN (McLAREN), 1M31.540S, 141.904MPH/228.373KPH, 2005

INSIDE TRACK
JAPANESE GRAND PRIX

Date:	**12 October**
Circuit name:	**Suzuka**
Circuit length:	**3.608 miles/5.806km**
Number of laps:	**53**
Email:	**info@suzukacircuit.com.jp**
Website:	**www.suzukacircuit.co.jp**

PREVIOUS WINNERS	
2002	**Michael Schumacher** FERRARI
2003	**Rubens Barrichello** FERRARI
2004	**Michael Schumacher** FERRARI
2005	**Kimi Raikkonen** McLAREN
2006	**Fernando Alonso** RENAULT
2009	**Sebastian Vettel** RED BULL
2010	**Sebastian Vettel** RED BULL
2011	**Jenson Button** McLAREN
2012	**Sebastian Vettel** RED BULL
2013	**Sebastian Vettel** RED BULL

F1 in Japan: Despite its burgeoning automobile industry and its rich motorbike racing heritage, Japan didn't land a Formula One grand prix until 1976. This was held in a thunderstorm at Fuji Speedway. After a second race there in 1977, Japan didn't hold another F1 grand prix until Suzuka took up the slot from 1987. TI Aida hosted an Asian GP in 1994 and 1995, while Fuji had a second go in 2007 and 2008.

Most successful Japanese driver: Aguri Suzuki was the first to claim a podium finish, for third place in the 1990 Japanese GP, a result matched in the 2004 United States GP by Takuma Sato and by Kamui Kobayashi in the 2012 Japanese GP.

Best corner: The two Degners, at the crest of the hill before the track crosses under its return leg, are very difficult, and they are made to feel claustrophobic as there's no space for any run-off outside these rapid righthanders with barriers close to the track.

Location: Honda selected this hillside site in the Shizuoka prefecture, just inland from the southern coast of Japan's main island, Honshu, when it wanted to build a circuit for testing purposes. It's 30 miles south-west of Nagoya, with the larger city of Osaka some 90 miles to the west.

SOCHI

For decades, Bernie Ecclestone has been determined to stage a grand prix in Russia and he has finally got his wish, albeit not in Moscow but on the streets of Sochi, a resort on the Black Sea.

Sochi on the Black Sea coast is a resort city in which President Putin is investing a considerable amount of money on prestige projects. First of all, he pitched successfully for it to host the Olympic Winter Games in early 2014. Then he clinched a deal to host a World Championship round on an all-new circuit built in the sporting complex forming the base for the Games, including facilities such as the skating and curling rinks.

The Sochi International Circuit is unusual for a street circuit as it has a lengthy lap. At 3.649 miles, it's the third longest on the F1 calendar after Spa-Francorchamps and Silverstone. It not only runs in and around

the Olympic Park, circling the main plaza, but heads off on a leg out towards the city's train station. In all, just over a mile of public roads are included in the lap.

There was much debate about whether this ground-breaking race would be included in the 2014 Formula One calendar or held back until 2015. This was because some of the construction work could not be started until after the conclusion of the Winter Games on 23 February, as it would cause too much disruption, and there were also questions about whether the finances would be in place and there's already talk of a circuit near Moscow taking over in the next few years.

"This place is incredible with the city, the sea and the mountains."
Sebastian Vettel

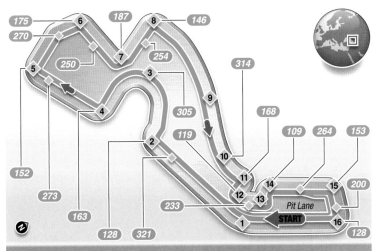

175 270 6 187 8 146
250 7 254
5 3 314
4 9
305 168
119 109 264 153
152 2 10
11 14 15 200
273 12 13 Pit Lane
163 233 START 16
128 321 128

111 *Km/H (simulated speeds)*

2013 POLE TIME: **NOT APPLICABLE**
2013 WINNER'S AVERAGE SPEED:
NOT APPLICABLE

2013 FASTEST LAP: **NOT APPLICABLE**
LAP RECORD: **NOT APPLICABLE**

INSIDE TRACK
RUSSIAN GRAND PRIX

Date:	5 October
Circuit name:	**Sochi International Circuit**
Circuit length:	**3.649 miles/5.872km**
Number of laps:	**52**
Email:	**N/A**
Website:	**N/A**

F1 in Russia: A Russian GP was held in St Petersburg in 1913 and 1914, but communism left the country on the sidelines. Before Sochi was chosen to hold the grand prix, Moscow had been talked about since 1983 as the likely place for it. These plans faltered several times. However, the capital city now has an international standard circuit of its own, the Moscow Raceway.

Most successful Russian driver: Vitaly Petrov holds this accolade by dint of being Russia's only F1 driver by the end of 2013. He scored 37 points for Renault in 2011, ranking 10th and finishing third in the season-opening Australian GP. He raced for Caterham in 2012 but lost his ride. This year, teenager Daniil Kvyat is stepping up from GP3 to drive for Toro Rosso, with Sergey Sirotkin lining up a ride with Sauber.

Best corner: Turn 2 looks to be where the action will be, with just a fast kink between it and the start line and a 90-degree right to negotiate on arrival.

Location: Sochi is on the north-eastern shore of the Black Sea, some 850 miles south of Moscow and just to the west of the country's border with Georgia.

An unusual structure: The ladder to the top of racing in Russia remains different, with its single-seater formulae no longer including F3. It doesn't even have Formula Renault but more rudimentary categories, as shown by Vitaly Petrov advancing through the Lada Cup for the country's small hatchbacks and then taking part in the Russian Formula 1600 Championship.

Gaining an international flavour: The opening of the Moscow Raceway has given Russian fans their first taste of the FIA World Touring Car Championship along with the European Formula Renault series.

CIRCUIT OF THE AMERICAS

This circuit outside Austin looked a hit from the moment the plans were published, and it has proved to be even better in the flesh with its exciting mix of gradient and fast bends.

The United States of America and Formula One have had a very on-off relationship, its grand prix flitting around the country ever since it was decided in 1980 that Watkins Glen was not modern enough, safe enough or close enough to a major city. Now, at last, the race appears to have found a home in Texas, with a brilliant circuit just outside Austin.

It's not just American fans who pack the grandstands here, as Mexico's reignited love of Formula One encourages many to cross the border for the event.

The lap starts with a climb every bit as steep as the one towards the first corner at the Red Bull Ring in Austria. The views from there over the circuit are epic. Then circuit designer Hermann Tilke has done his best with a wonderful section of sweeping esses before a fast kink and a hairpin, Turn 11. The drivers are then offered an even better chance to overtake down a long straight into tight Turn 12.

Sticking to his theme of combining the best corners from other circuits around the world, Tilke follows this with a slower, tighter section before it all opens out again for the lap's final few corners, with a good exit from the last of these crucial for a driver to get into position to catch a tow and thus create a chance of a passing move into Turn 1.

"Turns 2 to 8, with fast changes of direction, are special as you don't often see that on modern circuits." **Jenson Button**

90

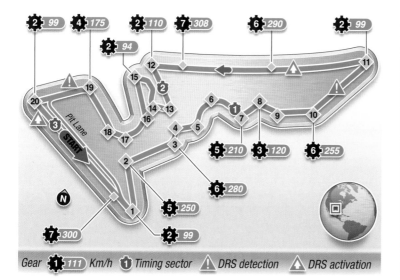

Gear **1** 111 Km/h **1** Timing sector ⚠ DRS detection ⚠ DRS activation

2013 POLE TIME: **VETTEL (RED BULL)**, 1M36.338S, 128.010MPH/206.012KPH
2013 WINNER'S AVERAGE SPEED: **115.807MPH/186.374KPH**

2013 FASTEST LAP: **VETTEL (RED BULL)**, 1M39.856S, 123.506MPH/198.764KPH
LAP RECORD: **VETTEL (RED BULL)**, 1M39.347S, 124.132KPH/199.772KPH, 2012

INSIDE TRACK
UNITED STATES GRAND PRIX

Date:	**9 November**
Circuit name:	**Circuit of the Americas**
Circuit length:	**3.400 miles/5.472km**
Number of laps:	**56**
Email:	info@circuitoftheamericas.com
Website:	www.circuitoftheamericas.com

PREVIOUS WINNERS

2012	**Lewis Hamilton** McLAREN
2013	**Sebastian Vettel** RED BULL

F1 in the USA: The United States GP has long been a race in search of a home. It was first held at Sebring in 1959, then immediately moved to California's Riverside. Watkins Glen in New York State was home from 1961 to 1980, then a race was held on the streets of Phoenix from 1989 to 1991, with an infield circuit at Indianapolis being used from 2000 to 2007. There were also other races on the streets of Long Beach, Dallas and Detroit.

Most successful American driver: There have been two American F1 World Champions, Phil Hill in 1961 for Ferrari and Mario Andretti in 1978 for Lotus. Andretti stands supreme, though, as he also won four Indycar titles and the Indianapolis 500.

Best corner: Turn 12 is the best place for overtaking after a long drag down from Turn 11, but the best place to watch the cars in action is undoubtedly the esses from Turn 3 to Turn 6, where the drivers have to really thread the needle at speed.

The next American: GP2 racer and occasional Caterham test driver Alexander Rossi has long been lined up to become the next American F1 racer after Scott Speed was dropped in 2007. However, GP3 race winner Conor Daly - son of Irish F1 racer Derek Daly - is hot on his heels.

A pass master: Lewis Hamilton's move to take the lead when Sebastian Vettel was blocked by a slower car in 2012 is the best move the circuit has seen yet.

Location: The circuit is eight miles south-east of the centre of Austin in central Texas. It was built on a hilly scrubland site and was the first in the USA to be purpose-built for F1.

INTERLAGOS

This is a circuit renowned for its exciting racing, and it has the added distinction of hosting the season's final grand prix, thus ensuring that its race action is given an extra twist.

The facilities may still be grubby and the paddock less than acceptable in standard, but Interlagos is very much a proper racing circuit. It dips, twists, rears up, flows and challenges from the start of the lap to the very end. Also, the burning passion that the Brazilian fans have for their racing, and especially for their heroes, ensures that Interlagos never operates with a less than electric, buzzing atmosphere. In many ways, this hillside autodrome has a gladiatorial feel to it, accentuated by the way that the drivers are hemmed in below high concrete walls in front of the grandstands before the start, the spectators looking down on the players.

To make the drivers even more tense before the start, the first corner has a blind exit as they arrive there at speed and anyone running wide can lose out as the track plunges to their left and feeds almost directly into the second bend.

A good lap here requires a driver to read the changing camber accurately, and nowhere is this more the case than when the drivers have negotiated Descida do Lago at the foot of the hill and started the up and down sequence of bends between Ferradura and Mergulho. Then, a clean exit from Juncao is essential as they try to accelerate as early as possible onto the curving start/finish straight.

INSIDE TRACK
BRAZILIAN GRAND PRIX

Date:	30 November
Circuit name:	Autodromo Jose Carlos Pace Interlagos
Circuit length:	2.667 miles/4.292km
Number of laps:	71
Email:	info@gpbrazil.com
Website:	www.gpbrazil.com

PREVIOUS WINNERS	
2004	**Juan Pablo Montoya** WILLIAMS
2005	**Juan Pablo Montoya** McLAREN
2006	**Felipe Massa** FERRARI
2007	**Kimi Raikkonen** FERRARI
2008	**Felipe Massa** FERRARI
2009	**Mark Webber** RED BULL
2010	**Sebastian Vettel** RED BULL
2011	**Mark Webber** RED BULL
2012	**Jenson Button** McLAREN
2013	**Sebastian Vettel** RED BULL

"The lap has a nice flow with a real variation of corners. There are fast sections, slow corners, elevation changes and off-camber parts of the lap. It has everything you need." **Paul di Resta**

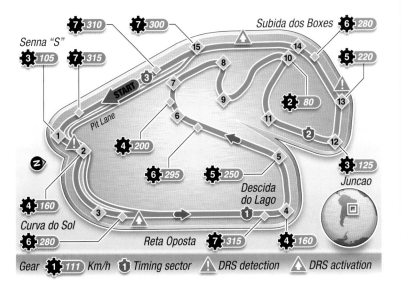

Senna "S"

Subida dos Boxes

START

Pit Lane

Descida do Lago

Juncao

Curva do Sol

Reta Oposta

Gear 🔘 111 Km/h 🔘 Timing sector ⚠ DRS detection ⚠ DRS activation

2013 POLE TIME: **VETTEL (RED BULL),** 1M26.479S, 111.459MPH/179.377KPH
2013 WINNER'S AVERAGE SPEED: **123.157MPH/198.202KPH**

2013 FASTEST LAP: **WEBBER (RED BULL),** 1M15.436S, 127.776MPH/205.636KPH
LAP RECORD: **MONTOYA (WILLIAMS),** 1M11.473S, 134.837MPH/217.000KPH, 2004

YAS MARINA

In complete contrast to the remote desert circuit of its neighbour Bahrain, Abu Dhabi's tailor-made venue is part of a sporting and leisure complex and offers some welcome glitz.

In the money-no-object Middle East, where the oil-rich nations are laying down culture and heritage, the Yas Marina Circuit impresses. How could it not? One look at the swish marina around which it's built, and especially the architecturally wild hotel that drapes itself over the track, tells you that this is more than your regular racing facility.

Hermann Tilke was given carte blanche and created a tight first corner to bunch the field, a sequence of esses to let the drivers tussle on the opening lap, then a chicane into a hairpin to let them jockey for position onto the long back straight. With a hairpin at its

end, this can offer a place to pass, especially with DRS and KERS, and another comes at the end of the arcing straight that follows down to Turn 11. The end of the lap is a bit stop/start in nature, but overall the circuit has a good flow and certainly offers a chance for the cars to hit impressive speeds, with nigh on 200mph seen before Turn 8.

While Singapore dazzles with its night race, Abu Dhabi, like Bahrain, gets to show off its sunset, with the race running as day turns to night, offering added spectacle as the lights come on around the central area of the track.

> "It's a very technical circuit with a lot of low-speed corners and you need to be extremely precise with the car." **Paul di Resta**

92

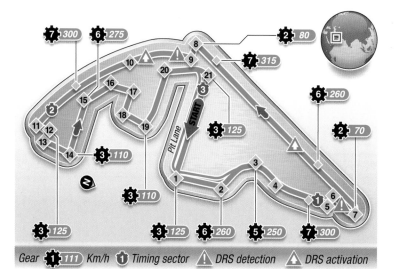

Gear 🔘 111 Km/h 🔘 Timing sector ⚠️ DRS detection ⚠️ DRS activation

2013 POLE TIME: **WEBBER (RED BULL),**
1M39.957S, 124.293MPH/200.030KPH
2013 WINNER'S AVERAGE SPEED:
116.046MPH/186.78KPH

2013 FASTEST LAP: **ALONSO (FERRARI),**
1M43.434S, 120.114MPH/193.305KPH
LAP RECORD: **VETTEL (RED BULL), 1M40.279S,**
131.387MPH/211.463KPH, 2009

INSIDE TRACK
ABU DHABI GRAND PRIX

Date:	**26 October**
Circuit name:	**Yas Marina Circuit**
Circuit length:	**3.451 miles/5.554km**
Number of laps:	**56**
Email:	
customerservice@yasmarinacircuit.com	
Website:	**www.yasmarinacircuit.com**

PREVIOUS WINNERS	
2009	**Sebastian Vettel** RED BULL
2010	**Sebastian Vettel** RED BULL
2011	**Lewis Hamilton** McLAREN
2012	**Kimi Raikkonen** LOTUS
2013	**Sebastian Vettel** RED BULL

Abu Dhabi's greatest race: The country's inaugural grand prix was disappointing, with a lack of overtaking, but the race in 2010 was far more exciting. It was the final round, and Sebastian Vettel hit the front and stayed there to sneak into the championship lead and so take the first of his F1 titles from under the nose of Ferrari's Fernando Alonso, the Spaniard losing time when he emerged from a pitstop to find himself stuck behind Vitaly Petrov's Renault for the remainder of the race.

Most successful Abu Dhabian driver: The country's most successful racing driver to date is Khaled Al Qubaisi, who has contested the Michelin Porsche Supercup series that supports the grands prix around Europe and last year raced in the Le Mans 24 Hours.

Best corner: The ability to brake as late as possible for Turn 8 at the end of the back straight and still line the car up for the left/right chicane that follows is key to gaining places here. Drivers have adapted their lines over the years, and watching the compromises they make in the heat of battle can be enthralling.

Location: The Yas Marina circuit was built on a plot on Abu Dhabi's Yas Island to the east of the capital of the wealthiest of the United Arab Emirates. Funded by Aldar Properties, this project includes the Ferrari World theme park, a water park, golf courses, polo fields and a marina.

The first three cars sit in finishing order in parc ferme in Abu Dhabi as Mark Webber, Sebastian Vettel and Nico Rosberg assemble on the podium above.

REVIEW OF THE 2013 SEASON

The end-of-season tally appears to offer only one summary of the 2013 World Championship, that Sebastian Vettel and Red Bull Racing destroyed the opposition. However, it was a season of two halves, with Red Bull initially pushed hard by Ferrari, Lotus and Mercedes. Then, after blow-outs forced Pirelli to change their tyres back to 2012 compounds, Red Bull re-established their dominance.

Sebastian Vettel was a worthy champion, and a four-time champion, as he was unrivalled for sustained pace in the races, able to strike hard and keep it up while the Mercedes drivers in particular found themselves going backwards, their race pace hardly ever matching their qualifying pace. Lewis Hamilton, in particular, was frustrated by having to back off in order to preserve his tyres.

Once Adrian Newey's chassis developments came on line and the 2012 tyre compounds were readopted, there was no stopping Vettel. He scored his first home win in the first race on the "old"

rubber, finished third behind Hamilton in Hungary, then won the remaining nine grands prix to set a record for the most consecutive wins in one season.

Team-mate Mark Webber was angered in Malaysia by Vettel ignoring team instructions not to overtake him, and so snatching victory. He was also unlucky to come up just short at the British GP, and bore the brunt of mechanical and operational glitches, but he leaves Formula One for sportscars with his head held high, having even usurped Hamilton for third overall at the final round.

With Red Bull in a class of their own, Ferrari and Mercedes spent the season battling to be best of the rest, with Fernando Alonso doing this almost on his own. His decision to air his frustrations about the team's relative lack of competitiveness mid-season may have worked against him as it prompted Ferrari to sign Kimi Raikkonen to race alongside him in 2014.

Mercedes displayed remarkable speed in qualifying in the first half of the season, bagging five of the nine poles up to the British GP, where Nico Rosberg added a somewhat fortuitous victory to his excellent one at Monaco. After the change of tyres, Hamilton was first home in Hungary, but that was as good as it got, as he then struggled to get the most out of his car before coming good at the final race to ensure that Mercedes ended the year second overall. Ferrari ought to have topped them, but Massa's points tally was insufficient to help them.

Lotus started the year with victory for Raikkonen in Australia, when most of the teams were at sea with their tyres. The Finn then gathered points when he could, but he was becoming increasingly disenchanted, as his wages were not being paid, and quit two races from the end of the year. By this point, Romain Grosjean had become the team's main focus and produced some stunning drives that were worthy of victory but went unrewarded.

There was then a massive gap back to McLaren, who suffered a truly awful season and failed to achieve a single podium finish,

their best being Jenson Button's fourth place at the final round. Disenchantment was in the air, not helped by technical director Paddy Lowe departing for Mercedes, and any progress made was stymied by the top teams also advancing. Sergio Perez came on strong at the end, but had not done enough to keep his 2014 drive.

Early in the season, the less well-funded Force India had the beating of McLaren, but this was one of the teams that lost its edge when the tyres were changed and it was only in the closing races that Paul di Resta and Adrian Sutil were able to challenge again, albeit both unsure as to whether they would keep their drives.

Conversely, Sauber benefited from the change in the tyres and Nico Hulkenberg underlined yet again why he is potentially the best of the lot, qualifying third at Monza and finishing fifth, then bettering that with fourth in Korea. Yet, as drivers with larger budgets have an advantage, he too ended the year unsure of which team he'd be driving for in 2014. He ended up at Force India.

Toro Rosso's duo impressed, with Daniel Ricciardo doing enough to land the coveted ride with Red Bull ahead of team-mate Jean-Eric Vergne by dint of his superior qualifying ability.

Williams gave up on its Coanda exhaust and Pastor Maldonado. Thanks to Jules Bianchi coming home 13th of the 16 finishers in Malaysia, Marussia went ahead of fellow non-scorers Caterham and, despite usually having the slower car, hung on to be classified 10th overall, to land that vital final portion of prize money.

AUSTRALIAN GP

The opening race of the season offered overtaking like almost never before in recent memory of Formula One, while the drop-off of tyre life was astonishingly swift. Yet through it all came super-smooth Kimi Raikkonen to win for Lotus.

Sole tyre supplier Pirelli had been instructed by Formula One's organizers to make the difference between its compounds more pronounced, to jazz up the racing. And this it most certainly did in Melbourne, although it left teams and pundits scratching their heads as to whether they had witnessed true form for the season ahead or a race that had been extraordinary.

Sebastian Vettel had opened his third title defence by dominating qualifying. Such was his pace, being 0.4s faster than team-mate Mark Webber, and 0.6s up on the best of the rest – Lewis Hamilton's Mercedes – that no one expected him not to win on the Sunday. In the end, he trailed home a well-beaten third. To make matters even more concerning for the German triple champion, his Red Bull had been beaten both by a Lotus and a Ferrari.

Vettel led away from the start, while team-mate Mark Webber had a poor start and fell from second to seventh. Amazingly, Vettel's supersoft tyres lost their performance so rapidly that he pitted for a set of mediums as early as lap 7. Felipe Massa took over the lead for Ferrari then came in a lap later, with Fernando Alonso taking over then pitting on lap 9. The Mercedes duo of Lewis Hamilton and Nico Rosberg moved to the front, and their F1 W04s were clearly kinder to their tyres as they stayed out for another five or six laps. Then, by dint of having started on medium compound tyres, Adrian Sutil led for Force India. Of course, he would have to fit supersofts later, with their rapid deterioration.

Once these stops had been made, Massa took the lead, but not for long, as he had to pit again. Alonso had come in a few laps earlier then run faster to move ahead not only of Massa but Sutil and Vettel too. Massa dropped to seventh.

This was nothing next to Raikkonen, though, as he stayed out a further 11 laps to make a two-stop strategy work and duly ascended to the lead as Alonso and Vettel had to make a third stop.

The ability to preserve tyres is one of Kimi Raikkonen's trademarks and it served him well.

MELBOURNE ROUND 1

DATE: 17 MARCH 2013

Laps: **58** • Distance: **191.126 miles/307.588km** • Weather: **Damp then dry**

Pos	Driver	Team	Result	Stops	Qualifying Time	Grid
1	**Kimi Raikkonen**	Lotus	1h30m03.225s	2	1m28.738s	7
2	**Fernando Alonso**	Ferrari	1h30m15.676s	3	1m28.493s	5
3	**Sebastian Vettel**	Red Bull	1h30m25.571s	3	1m27.407s	1
4	**Felipe Massa**	Ferrari	1h30m36.802s	3	1m28.490s	4
5	**Lewis Hamilton**	Mercedes	1h30m48.786s	3	1m28.087s	3
6	**Mark Webber**	Red Bull	1h30m50.025s	3	1m27.827s	2
7	**Adrian Sutil**	Force India	1h31m08.293s	2	1m38.134s	12
8	**Paul di Resta**	Force India	1h31m11.674s	2	1m29.305s	9
9	**Jenson Button**	McLaren	1h31m24.855s	3	1m30.357s	10
10	**Romain Grosjean**	Lotus	1h31m25.984s	3	1m29.013s	8
11	**Sergio Perez**	McLaren	1h31m26.592s	3	1m39.900s	15
12	**Jean-Eric Vergne**	Toro Rosso	1h31m27.082s	3	1m38.778s	13
13	**Esteban Gutierrez**	Sauber	57 laps	2	1m47.776s	18
14	**Valtteri Bottas**	Williams	57 laps	3	1m40.290s	16
15	**Jules Bianchi**	Marussia	57 laps	3	1m48.147s	19
16	**Charles Pic**	Caterham	56 laps	2	1m50.626s	22
17	**Max Chilton**	Marussia	56 laps	3	1m48.909s	20
18	**Giedo van der Garde**	Caterham	56 laps	3	1m49.519s	21
R	**Daniel Ricciardo**	Toro Rosso	39 laps/exhaust	2	1m39.042s	14
R	**Nico Rosberg**	Mercedes	26 laps/electrics	1	1m28.523s	6
R	**Pastor Maldonado**	Williams	24 laps/spun off	1	1m47.614s	17
R	**Nico Hulkenberg**	Sauber	0 laps/fuel leak	-	1m38.067s	11

FASTEST LAP: RAIKKONEN, 1M29.274S, 132.883MPH/213.855KPH ON LAP 56 • **RACE LEADERS:** VETTEL 1-6; MASSA 7, 21-22; ALONSO 8, 34-38; HAMILTON 9-12; ROSBERG 13; SUTIL 14-20, 39-42; RAIKKONEN 23-33, 43-58

The fragile relationship between Red Bull team-mates Sebastian Vettel and Mark Webber imploded when Vettel ignored team orders to hold station and overtook Webber, who was sticking to instructions to turn his engine down and preserve his tyres, to claim a controversial win.

Formula One fans have become accustomed to seeing Sebastian Vettel smiling and celebrating, such has been his extraordinary run of success since 2009 as he gathered three drivers' titles in succession. However, at Sepang he showed the other side of his character, the one that will seek victory at all costs. The net result was his 27th F1 win – equalling Jackie Stewart's tally – a massively disgruntled Webber and the undermining of team principal Christian Horner.

The track was wet for the start of the race and Vettel led away from the grid, but he decided that it was drying fast enough for slicks to be fitted and so came in on lap 5, letting Webber move to the front. The Australian stayed out two laps longer and retook the lead when he rejoined. And this was how it stayed until the start of lap 44 when, with no opposition running close enough to prevent a Red Bull one-two finish, as Lewis Hamilton was dropping his pace to preserve fuel, both Webber and Vettel were instructed to "Multi 21". This meant to back off, save their tyres and remain as per their race order. The trouble was, Vettel felt that he was the faster of the pair on a new set of option tyres saved from the day before and he wanted to make the most of them. He kept closing on Webber, ignoring pleas from Horner "not to be silly", then used the double advantage offered by his KERS and DRS to force his way past as they raced into Turn 1 on lap 46. Webber fought back through Turn 2, but Vettel made it in front for good at Turn 4. Quite naturally, Webber was livid and raged at Vettel before they went onto the podium. Afterwards, Vettel apologized, but that went no way towards undoing the damage done.

Hamilton was able to finish not far behind in third, with team-mate Nico Rosberg right on his tail. In this pairing, it was Rosberg who was upset, but that was because he respected team orders to hold position and so had to make do with fourth place rather than force his way through to third.

SEPANG ROUND 2

DATE: 24 MARCH 2013

Laps: **56** • Distance: **192.888 miles/310.424km** • Weather: **Damp then dry**

Pos	Driver	Team	Result	Stops	Qualifying Time	Grid
1	**Sebastian Vettel**	Red Bull	1h38m56.681s	4	1m49.674s	1
2	**Mark Webber**	Red Bull	1h39m00.979s	4	1m52.244s	5
3	**Lewis Hamilton**	Mercedes	1h39m08.862s	4	1m51.699s	4
4	**Nico Rosberg**	Mercedes	1h39m09.321s	4	1m52.519s	6
5	**Felipe Massa**	Ferrari	1h39m22.329s	4	1m50.587s	2
6	**Romain Grosjean**	Lotus	1h39m32.245s	3	1m37.636s	11
7	**Kimi Raikkonen**	Lotus	1h39m45.160s	3	1m52.970s	10*
8	**Nico Hulkenberg**	Sauber	1h39m49.725s	4	1m38.125s	12
9	**Sergio Perez**	McLaren	1h40m09.038s	4	1m54.136s	9
10	**Jean-Eric Vergne**	Toro Rosso	1h40m23.805s	3	1m38.157s	17
11	**Valtteri Bottas**	Williams	1h40m25.291s	3	1m38.207s	18
12	**Esteban Gutierrez**	Sauber	55 laps	4	1m39.221s	14
13	**Jules Bianchi**	Marussia	55 laps	4	1m38.434s	19
14	**Charles Pic**	Caterham	55 laps	4	1m39.314s	20
15	**Giedo van der Garde**	Caterham	55 laps	4	1m39.932s	21
16	**Max Chilton**	Marussia	54 laps	4	1m39.672s	21
17	**Jenson Button**	McLaren	53 laps/vibration	3	1m53.175s	7
18	**Daniel Ricciardo**	Toro Rosso	51 laps/exhaust	3	1m38.822s	13
R	**Pastor Maldonado**	Williams	45 laps/KERS	3	No time	16
R	**Adrian Sutil**	Force India	27 laps/wheelnuts	2	1m53.439s	8
R	**Paul di Resta**	Force India	22 laps/wheelnuts	2	1m44.509s	15
R	**Fernando Alonso**	Ferrari	1 lap/accident	0	1m50.727s	3

FASTEST LAP: PEREZ, 1M39.199S, 125.000MPH/201.168KPH ON LAP 56 • **RACE LEADERS:** VETTEL 1-4, 19-22, 31-32, 46-56; WEBBER 5-7, 9-18, 23-30, 35-45; ROSBERG 8; BUTTON 33-34 • * 3-PLACE GRID PENALTY FOR IMPEDING ROSBERG

Mark Webber leads a Red Bull one-two and was livid that the order was reversed by the end.

Fernando Alonso gave himself a points boost by racing to victory in Shanghai, but the race was just as much one for the teams' tacticians on the pitwall as they plotted just when and how hard their drivers could push.

Lewis Hamilton qualified on pole position, his first for Mercedes, and led for four laps, but then, in an instant, he was demoted. Not just by Fernando Alonso's Ferrari, but also the second Ferrari of Felipe Massa, both flashing past him on the rush towards Turn 1.

The TV images beamed globally of this double passing manoeuvre, one passing on either side of the Silver Arrow, suggested great racing, but even at this early stage the race was one of high-speed chess. Hamilton pitted at the end of that lap, swapping his soft tyres for mediums, and the Ferraris soon followed suit. This left Sebastian Vettel leading from Sauber's Nico Hulkenberg, until they both pitted on lap 15.

Having qualified eighth, Jenson Button knew that he had to gamble, and his gamble was to start on medium tyres and to go as long as he could on those. Thus he took over the lead and remained there until passed by Alonso on lap 21. A few laps later, Button pitted from second, coming in as Alonso dived for the pits again, and so it was clear that the McLaren driver was planning to stop twice as opposed to the three pit visits his leading rivals were expected to make.

Vettel was out of synch with Alonso, making his second stop eight laps after the Spaniard's, on lap 31, at which point onlookers realized the success of their respective tactics would only become apparent in the closing laps. Alonso then showed that he was the man to beat when he overtook Vettel for the lead on lap 29 and then again just after his third stop.

The big question at this point was how long Vettel could make his medium tyres last before fitting softs. The answer was until five laps from the end. By the time he came out again, he was fourth behind Kimi Raikkonen's Lotus and Hamilton. He then flew towards Hamilton but ran wide around a backmarker, which left him too far back to be able to engage DRS for the final run down the back straight and so he ended up fourth.

Fernando Alonso made it three winners in the first three rounds in another strategy-led race.

SHANGHAI ROUND 3

DATE: **14 APRIL 2013**

Laps: **56** • Distance: **189.568 miles/305.081km** • Weather: **Warm & dry**

Pos	Driver	Team	Result	Stops	Qualifying Time	Grid
1	**Fernando Alonso**	Ferrari	1h36m26.945s	3	1m34.788s	3
2	**Kimi Raikkonen**	Lotus	1h36m37.113s	3	1m34.761s	2
3	**Lewis Hamilton**	Mercedes	1h36m39.267s	3	1m34.484s	1
4	**Sebastian Vettel**	Red Bull	1h36m39.470s	3	No time	9
5	**Jenson Button**	McLaren	1h37m02.230s	2	2m05.673s	8
6	**Felipe Massa**	Ferrari	1h37m18.029s	3	1m34.933s	5
7	**Daniel Ricciardo**	Toro Rosso	1h37m09.636s	3	1m35.998s	7
8	**Paul di Resta**	Force India	1h37m18.029s	3	1m36.287s	11
9	**Romain Grosjean**	Lotus	1h37m20.368s	3	1m35.364s	6
10	**Nico Hulkenberg**	Sauber	1h37m23.543s	3	No time	10
11	**Sergio Perez**	McLaren	1h37m30.805s	2	1m36.314s	12
12	**Jean-Eric Vergne**	Toro Rosso	1h37m39.549s	3	1m37.199s	15
13	**Valtteri Bottas**	Williams	1h38m00.806s	3	1m37.769s	16
14	**Pastor Maldonado**	Williams	1h38m02.398s	3	1m37.139s	14
15	**Jules Bianchi**	Marussia	55 laps	3	1m38.780s	18
16	**Charles Pic**	Caterham	55 laps	3	1m39.614s	20
17	**Max Chilton**	Marussia	55 laps	3	1m39.537s	19
18	**Giedo van der Garde**	Caterham	55 laps	3	1m39.660s	21
R	**Nico Rosberg**	Mercedes	21 laps/anti-roll bar	3	1m34.861s	4
R	**Mark Webber**	Red Bull	15 laps/lost wheel	2	-	22*
R	**Adrian Sutil**	Force India	5 laps/crash damage	0	1m36.405s	13
R	**Esteban Gutierrez**	Sauber	4 laps/accident	0	1m37.990s	17

FASTEST LAP: VETTEL, 1M36.808S, 125.962MPH/202.717KPH ON LAP 53 • **RACE LEADERS:** HAMILTON 1-4; ALONSO 5, 21-23, 29-41, 43-56; MASSA 6; VETTEL 7-14, 24-28, 42; BUTTON 15-20 • * EXCLUDED FROM QUALIFYING FOR NOT HAVING ENOUGH FUEL

BAHRAIN GP

If Red Bull Racing got its tyre choices wrong in China, it got them spot on in Bahrain to enable Sebastian Vettel to win as he pleased and so open out a 10-point lead over the driver who chased him home, Kimi Raikkonen.

There have been days during the illustrious Sebastian Vettel-Red Bull Racing partnership when they have been in a different class to their opposition, and this was one such day.

Vettel had been beaten to pole position by Nico Rosberg's Mercedes, but this didn't worry him unduly as the Mercedes was a car that still ate its tyres quickly, making its qualifying performances flatter to deceive.

On the opening lap Vettel warded off a concerted attack from Ferrari's Fernando Alonso all the way to the exit of the fast sweepers halfway around the lap and then tucked into his fellow German's slipstream to wait until the moment was right to take the lead from him. This came at Turn 4 on the third lap and he then pulled easily clear, the Mercedes already struggling with overheating tyres. Recognizing this, Alonso closed in and attacked Rosberg, getting clear on lap 5 after a good scrap.

The race changed when Vettel pitted from the lead on lap 10, as Paul di Resta took over the lead in his Force India. He pitted four laps later and this put Kimi Raikkonen out front. With the Lotus so light on its tyres, the Finn planned to pit only twice, making his first stop on lap 16.

Vettel regained the lead at this point and was never to be headed, his form so dominant that it was clear that no one could live with him, not even team-mate Mark Webber who'd had a three-place grid penalty then lost too much time in traffic.

The closest challengers turned out to be the Lotus duo, but Raikkonen was 9s adrift at the finish, with Romain Grosjean another 10s back after overhauling di Resta late in the race. Webber looked to be on course for fifth, but his tyres were finished and he fell two places on the final lap as Lewis Hamilton and Sergio Perez demoted him. The Mexican had had an intra-team battle with Jenson Button until the Englishman was forced to make a fourth stop for tyres, which dropped him to a disappointed and angry 10th overall.

SAKHIR ROUND 4

DATE: **21 APRIL 2013**

Laps: 57 • Distance: **191.580 miles/308.319km** • Weather: **Hot & bright**

Pos	Driver	Team	Result	Stops	Qualifying Time	Grid
1	Sebastian Vettel	Red Bull	1h36m00.498s	3	1m32.584s	2
2	Kimi Raikkonen	Lotus	1h36m09.609s	2	1m33.327s	8
3	Romain Grosjean	Lotus	1h36m20.005s	3	1m33.762s	11
4	Paul di Resta	Force India	1h36m22.225s	2	1m33.235s	5
5	Lewis Hamilton	Mercedes	1h36m35.728s	3	1m32.762s	9**
6	Sergio Perez	McLaren	1h36m36.496s	3	1m33.914s	12
7	Mark Webber	Red Bull	1h36m37.742s	3	1m33.078s	7*
8	Fernando Alonso	Ferrari	1h36m38.072s	4	1m32.667s	3
9	Nico Rosberg	Mercedes	1h36m41.624s	4	1m32.330s	1
10	Jenson Button	McLaren	1h36m47.129s	4	No time	10
11	Pastor Maldonado	Williams	1h37m06.948s	3	1m34.425s	17
12	Nico Hulkenberg	Sauber	1h37m13.431s	3	1m33.976s	14
13	Adrian Sutil	Force India	1h37m17.217s	3	1m33.246s	6
14	Valtteri Bottas	Williams	1h37m22.009s	3	1m34.105s	15
15	Felipe Massa	Ferrari	1h37m26.862s	4	1m33.207s	4
16	Daniel Ricciardo	Toro Rosso	56 laps	3	1m33.974s	13
17	Charles Pic	Caterham	56 laps	3	1m35.283s	18
18	Esteban Gutierrez	Sauber	56 laps	4	1m34.730s	24!
19	Jules Bianchi	Marussia	56 laps	4	1m36.178s	19
20	Max Chilton	Marussia	56 laps	4	1m36.476s	21
21	Giedo van der Garde	Caterham	55 laps	5	1m36.304s	20
R	Jean-Eric Vergne	Toro Rosso	16 laps/crash damage	1	1m34.284s	16

FASTEST LAP: VETTEL, 1M36.961S, 119.696MPH/200.938KPH ON LAP 55 • **RACE LEADERS:** ROSBERG 1-2; VETTEL 3-10, 15-57; DI RESTA 11-13; RAIKKONEN 14 • *3-PLACE GRID PENALTY FOR CAUSING A COLLISION • **5-PLACE GRID PENALTY FOR GEARBOX CHANGE • ! 5-PLACE GRID PENALTY FOR CAUSING A COLLISION

Sebastian Vettel got the best out of the Pirelli tyres in the heat of Bahrain on race day.

SPANISH GP

Ferrari reckoned that a four-stop race strategy would work best for Fernando Alonso, and this complex strategic decision did just that, allowing the Spaniard to score his second home win, with his 2014 team-mate Kimi Raikkonen taking third place for the third time in a row.

Mercedes claimed its third pole in succession, but Red Bull Racing, Lotus and Ferrari paid little attention to this, as they expected the Silver Arrows to suffer their regular fate of failing to make their tyres last long enough in the race to be able to push hard.

Nico Rosberg knew that his fate was to slide backwards down the race order, and this he did after he made the first of his three pitstops on lap 10. Team-mate Lewis Hamilton had lined up behind him but had Vettel swoop around the outside of him at the first corner as Rosberg braked slightly early and caused those behind to bunch up. Crucially, Hamilton locked up and flat-spotted one of his front tyres in avoidance. Then Alonso struck as Hamilton scrapped for position with Kimi Raikkonen and went past both around the outside of Turn 3. Five laps later, Raikkonen also passed Hamilton, who fell away, saying that he could find no grip. He would end the day 12th and would later describe his race as "one of the worst I've had".

Alonso pitted on lap 9 and he moved ahead of Vettel after the German stopped on the following lap. He then caught Rosberg, who had also pitted, and the pair began to drop Vettel off their tail. Then, on lap 13, the Spaniard sent the crowd into a frenzy as he passed the Mercedes on the start/finish straight. Rosberg's race then fell apart, as by Turn 5 Vettel and Massa had got past too.

From there on, Alonso was in the driving seat, and the story of the remainder of the race was the way that Rosberg continued to go backwards while Raikkonen had the opposite fortune and worked his way through to second by dint of stopping three times to his rivals' four, eventually pushing Massa back to third when the Brazilian made his final pitstop on lap 51.

At the end of the day, while everyone applauded Alonso and Ferrari for their winning strategy, perhaps the biggest pat on the back should have gone to the 11 pitcrews, who between them completed 77 pitstops.

Any win is good, but for Fernando Alonso this was a special one, his second Spanish GP win.

BARCELONA ROUND 5

DATE: 12 MAY 2013

Laps: 66 • Distance: **190.904 miles/307.231km** • Weather: **Sunny & warm**

Pos	Driver	Team	Result	Stops	Qualifying Time	Grid
1	**Fernando Alonso**	Ferrari	1h39m16.596s	4	1m21.218s	5
2	**Kimi Raikkonen**	Lotus	1h39m25.934s	3	1m21.177s	4
3	**Felipe Massa**	Ferrari	1h39m42.645s	4	1m21.219s	9*
4	**Sebastian Vettel**	Red Bull	1h39m54.869s	4	1m21.054s	3
5	**Mark Webber**	Red Bull	1h40m04.559s	4	1m21.570s	7
6	**Nico Rosberg**	Mercedes	1h40m24.616s	3	1m20.718s	1
7	**Paul di Resta**	Force India	1h40m25.584s	4	1m22.233s	10
8	**Jenson Button**	McLaren	1h40m36.102s	4	1m22.355s	14
9	**Sergio Perez**	McLaren	1h40m38.334s	4	1m22.069s	8
10	**Daniel Ricciardo**	Toro Rosso	65 laps	4	1m22.127s	11
11	**Esteban Gutierrez**	Sauber	65 laps	4	1m22.793s	19*
12	**Lewis Hamilton**	Mercedes	65 laps	4	1m20.972s	2
13	**Adrian Sutil**	Force India	65 laps	4	1m22.346s	13
14	**Pastor Maldonado**	Williams	65 laps	4	1m23.318s	17
15	**Nico Hulkenberg**	Sauber	65 laps	5	1m22.389s	15
16	**Valtteri Bottas**	Williams	65 laps	3	1m23.260s	16
17	**Charles Pic**	Caterham	65 laps	3	1m25.070s	22
18	**Jules Bianchi**	Marussia	64 laps	4	1m24.713s	20
19	**Max Chilton**	Marussia	64 laps	3	1m24.996s	21
R	**Jean-Eric Vergne**	Toro Rosso	52 laps/crash damage	4	1m22.166s	12
R	**Giedo van der Garde**	Caterham	21 laps/lost wheel	2	1m24.661s	18
R	**Romain Grosjean**	Lotus	8 laps/suspension	0	1m21.308s	6

FASTEST LAP: GUTIERREZ, 1M26.217S, 120.776MPH/194.370KPH ON LAP 56 • RACE LEADERS: ROSBERG 1-10; GUTIERREZ 11-12; ALONSO 13-21, 26-36, 39-66; VETTEL 22-23; RAIKKONEN 24-25, 37-38 • * 3-PLACE GRID PENALTY FOR IMPEDING

MONACO GP

The Monaco GP almost always provides something different, and it certainly did in 2013 for Mercedes as the team that had struggled to make its tyres last during the early season races came out on top after Nico Rosberg produced a flawless drive.

Mercedes' season had been long on promise but short on results when Nico Rosberg and Lewis Hamilton arrived in Monaco for the grand prix. Their cars simply took too much out of their tyres to stay on the pace throughout a race distance. They reckoned, though, that this street circuit ought to offer them more of a chance due to its lack of tyre-burning high-speed corners.

Rosberg and Hamilton duly made the most of the F1 W04s' one-lap speed and locked out the front row. They then did the next critical thing, exiting Ste Devote first and second on the opening lap, Rosberg ahead of Hamilton. And then, from there, they dictated the race, thus being able to run at a slower pace than they otherwise would, knowing that it was unlikely anyone would be able to pass them thanks to the almost total lack of overtaking places.

Yet the day didn't go totally Mercedes' way, as a safety car period was triggered on lap 30 by Felipe Massa repeating an accident he had had at Ste Devote in practice, and this meant that Hamilton had to pit on the same lap as Rosberg. He was asked to delay his arrival by 6s so that the German would be clear of the pit and his own new tyres ready, but he hung back by more like 11s and this dropped him behind the Red Bulls when he rejoined. Once there, Hamilton could find no way back past, and he was consigned to a frustrated fourth.

There was a further safety car period late in the race when Max Chilton failed to notice Pastor Maldonado coming up to lap him and moved his Marussia to the right, dispatching the Williams into the barriers at Tabac, fortunately without injury to the Venezuelan.

The one dark cloud on this great day for Mercedes came after the race, when Red Bull and Ferrari protested the result, saying that a tyre test that the team had conducted in secret for Pirelli after the Spanish GP had given them an unfair advantage. The team was later forced to miss the young driver test after the British GP as a punishment.

MONACO ROUND 6

DATE: **21 APRIL 2013**

Laps: 78 • Distance: **161.155 miles/259.354km** • Weather: **Warm & sunny**

Pos	Driver	Team	Result	Stops	Qualifying Time	Grid
1	**Nico Rosberg**	Mercedes	2h17m52.056s	1	1m13.876s	1
2	**Sebastian Vettel**	Red Bull	2h17m55.944s	1	1m13.980s	3
3	**Mark Webber**	Red Bull	2h17m58.370s	1	1m14.181s	4
4	**Lewis Hamilton**	Mercedes	2h18m05.950s	1	1m13.967s	2
5	**Adrian Sutil**	Force India	2h18m13.533s	1	1m15.383s	8
6	**Jenson Button**	McLaren	2h18m15.159s	1	1m15.647s	9
7	**Fernando Alonso**	Ferrari	2h18m18.790s	1	1m14.824s	6
8	**Jean-Eric Vergne**	Toro Rosso	2h18m19.279s	1	1m15.703s	10
9	**Paul di Resta**	Force India	2h18m19.644s	1	1m26.322s	17
10	**Kimi Raikkonen**	Lotus	2h18m28.638s	2	1m14.822s	5
11	**Nico Hulkenberg**	Sauber	2h18m34.628s	1	1m18.331s	11
12	**Valtteri Bottas**	Williams	2h18m34.747s	1	1m19.077s	14
13	**Esteban Gutierrez**	Sauber	2h18m35.268s	2	1m26.917s	19
14	**Max Chilton**	Marussia	2h18m41.941s	2	1m27.203s	22*
15	**Giedo van der Garde**	Caterham	2h18m54.646s	3	1m19.408s	15
16	**Sergio Perez**	McLaren	72 laps/brakes	1	1m15.138s	7
R	**Romain Grosjean**	Lotus	63 laps/crash damage	2	1m18.603s	13
R	**Daniel Ricciardo**	Toro Rosso	61 laps/accident	1	1m18.344s	12
R	**Jules Bianchi**	Marussia	58 laps/brakes	2	No time	20
R	**Pastor Maldonado**	Williams	44 laps/accident	1	1m21.688s	16
R	**Felipe Massa**	Ferrari	28 laps/suspension	1	No time	21*
R	**Charles Pic**	Caterham	7 laps/gearbox	0	1m26.633s	18

FASTEST LAP: VETTEL, 1M16.577S, 97.566MPH/157.018KPH ON LAP 77 • **RACE LEADERS:** ROSBERG 1-78 • * 5-PLACE GRID PENALTY FOR GEARBOX CHANGE

Mercedes' Nico Rosberg leads into Ste Devote, followed by Hamilton, Vettel and Webber.

Sebastian Vettel bows to his Red Bull RB9 in tribute after his victory in the Indian GP resulted in his fourth consecutive drivers' title.

CANADIAN GP

Sebastian Vettel secured his third win of 2014 on a day when neither Ferrari nor Mercedes could match his pace in an unusually undramatic race. The ease with which Vettel won made many think that he could now make it four titles in a row.

The statistics of Sebastian Vettel's 2014 Canadian GP read like this: pole position - breaking Mercedes' grip on qualifying; leading from the start and staying in front for all but two of the laps, when he lost the lead while taking his first pitstop; then taking the chequered flag 14s to the good for his 29th win. The reality was probably even more dominant than those figures suggest, as Red Bull Racing truly hit top form.

Vettel had bagged pole by only a narrow margin over Mercedes' Lewis Hamilton, but he made the most of the prime starting position to lead both into and more importantly out of the first corner. He was already 2s clear by the end of the opening lap and it was clear that he was pushing hard to build an advantage, but he almost came unstuck on lap 10 when he clipped one of the surrounding walls and was fortunate not to damage his car. He would later have another moment when he ran off track at the first corner late in the race, but nobody was going to deny him his victory.

Hamilton might have reckoned that he was all set for second place, but this became third when Fernando Alonso powered past with eight laps to go. The Spaniard had worked his way forward from sixth on the grid and picked off surprise third fastest qualifier Valtteri Bottas, Nico Rosberg and Mark Webber along the way. The Australian had been hampered a few laps before Alonso came past into the first corner by a collision with Giedo van der Garde's Caterham at the hairpin that left his Red Bull missing a winglet from his front wing.

One of the drives of the race came from Paul di Resta who started his Force India 17th, yet his first set of tyres were mediums and he made these last so well that he pitted only once, to change to the supersofts, and again made them last so well that he finished seventh.

Tragically, a marshal was killed when a crane that was recovering Esteban Gutierrez's crashed Sauber ran him over.

F1's three best drivers - Vettel, Alonso and Hamilton - share the Montreal podium.

MONTREAL ROUND 7
DATE: **9 JUNE 2013**

Laps: **70** • Distance: **189.686 miles/305.271km** • Weather: **Warm & sunny**

Pos	Driver	Team	Result	Stops	Qualifying Time	Grid
1	Sebastian Vettel	Red Bull	1h32m09.143s	2	1m25.425s	1
2	Fernando Alonso	Ferrari	1h32m23.551s	2	1m26.504s	6
3	Lewis Hamilton	Mercedes	1h32m25.085s	2	1m25.512s	2
4	Mark Webber	Red Bull	1h32m34.874s	2	1m26.208s	5
5	Nico Rosberg	Mercedes	1h33m18.868s	3	1m26.008s	4
6	Jean-Eric Vergne	Toro Rosso	69 laps	2	1m26.543s	7
7	Paul di Resta	Force India	69 laps	1	1m24.908s	17
8	Felipe Massa	Ferrari	69 laps	2	1m30.354s	16
9	Kimi Raikkonen	Lotus	69 laps	1	1m27.432s	10*
10	Adrian Sutil	Force India	69 laps	2	1m27.348s	8
11	Sergio Perez	McLaren	69 laps	2	1m29.761s	12
12	Jenson Button	McLaren	69 laps	1	1m30.068s	14
13	Romain Grosjean	Lotus	69 laps	2	1m25.716s	22**
14	Valtteri Bottas	Williams	69 laps	2	1m25.897s	3
15	Daniel Ricciardo	Toro Rosso	68 laps	2	1m27.946s	11*
16	Pastor Maldonado	Williams	68 laps	2	1m29.917s	13
17	Jules Bianchi	Marussia	68 laps	1	1m26.508s	19
18	Charles Pic	Caterham	67 laps	2	1m25.626s	18
19	Max Chilton	Marussia	67 laps	1	1m27.062s	20
20	Esteban Gutierrez	Sauber	63 laps/accident	2	1m30.315s	15
R	Nico Hulkenberg	Sauber	45 laps/crash damage	2	1m29.435s	9
R	Giedo van der Garde	Caterham	43 laps/crash damage	3	1m27.110s	21

FASTEST LAP: WEBBER, 1M16.182S, 128.052MPH/206.080KPH ON LAP 69 • **RACE LEADERS:** VETTEL 1-15, 19-70; HAMILTON16-18 • * EXCLUDED FROM QUALIFYING FOR NOT HAVING ENOUGH FUEL • ** 10-PLACE GRID PENALTY FOR CAUSING A COLLISION

BRITISH GP

Everyone was talking about tyres after this extraordinary race at Silverstone, for they exploded with frightening regularity at various points around this high-speed circuit and cost Lewis Hamilton a win that went instead to Mercedes team-mate Nico Rosberg.

Tyres had been at the centre of every F1 discussion at the start of the season, but this had largely died down ... until the British GP. What unfolded in the race was extraordinary and frankly dangerous, as there were no fewer than four blow-outs, something that was a major concern on such a high-speed circuit. Red Bull technical chief Adrian Newey said that the sport had had a "narrow escape".

Lewis Hamilton led a Mercedes one-two on the grid. Next up were the Red Bulls, then Daniel Ricciardo after a fantastic lap for Toro Rosso followed by Adrian Sutil for Force India, ahead of the Lotus duo. Paul di Resta had lapped fast enough to be fifth in the other Force India, but his car was underweight so he was put to the back of the grid. It's not often that you have to look to the fifth row for the faster of the Ferraris, but that's where Fernando Alonso ended up, ahead of McLaren's disgruntled Jenson Button.

Hamilton made a good enough start to lead away ahead of Vettel, who had jumped Rosberg, until Hamilton's left rear tyre exploded on the Wellington Straight on lap 8. He controlled the moment and limped back to the pits. His recovery drive from there was remarkable as, aided by two safety car periods, he made it back to fourth place.

Two laps later, Felipe Massa suffered the same fate at Aintree, where he spun after a sudden deflation. Team-mate Alonso also suffered the same fate at the last corner and pitted immediately.

With Hamilton out of the reckoning, Vettel had the race in his pocket. Then, on lap 41, his gearbox failed. The excitement in the closing laps was provided by Mark Webber catching the Mercedes, no doubt cursing another terrible start that had dropped him to 14th. At flagfall, he was just 0.765s adrift. Fernando Alonso was lucky to finish third, given that he had a moment of drama; with Sergio Perez in front of him as they flew down the Hangar Straight, a tyre blew on the McLaren and it took true skill to avoid the flailing rubber.

SILVERSTONE ROUND 8
DATE: 30 JUNE 2013

Laps: **52** • Distance: **190.271 miles/306.212km** • Weather: **Warm & sunny**

Pos	Driver	Team	Result	Stops	Qualifying Time	Grid
1	Nico Rosberg	Mercedes	1h32m59.531s	3	1m30.059s	2
2	Mark Webber	Red Bull	1h33m00.221s	3	1m30.220s	4
3	Fernando Alonso	Ferrari	1h33m06.580s	3	1m30.979s	9
4	Lewis Hamilton	Mercedes	1h33m07.212s	2	1m29.607s	1
5	Kimi Raikkonen	Lotus	1h33m10.713s	2	1m30.962s	8
6	Felipe Massa	Ferrari	1h33m14.029s	4	1m31.779s	11
7	Adrian Sutil	Force India	1h33m15.791s	2	1m20.908s	6
8	Daniel Ricciardo	Toro Rosso	1h33m15.999s	2	1m30.757s	5
9	Paul di Resta	Force India	1h33m17.399s	3	No time	21*
10	Nico Hulkenberg	Sauber	1h33m19.165s	3	1m32.211s	14
11	Pastor Maldonado	Williams	1h33m20.591s	2	1m32.359s	15
12	Valtteri Bottas	Williams	1h33m24.550s	2	1m32.664	16
13	Jenson Button	McLaren	1h33m25.425s	2	1m31.649s	10
14	Esteban Gutierrez	Sauber	1h33m25.741s	4	1m32.666s	17
15	Charles Pic	Caterham	1h33m31.069s	2	1m33.866s	18
16	Jules Bianchi	Marussia	1h33m35.553s	2	1m34.108s	19
17	Max Chilton	Marussia	1h34m07.116s	2	1m35.858s	20
18	Giedo van der Garde	Caterham	1h34m07.215s	3	1m35.481s	22**
19	Romain Grosjean	Lotus	51 laps/front wing	3	1m30.955s	7
20	Sergio Perez	McLaren	46 laps/tyre failure	2	1m32.082s	13
R	Sebastian Vettel	Red Bull	41 laps/gearbox	2	1m30.211s	3
R	Jean-Eric Vergne	Toro Rosso	35 laps/tyre failure	2	1m31.785s	12

FASTEST LAP: WEBBER, 1M33.401S, 141.094MPH/227.069KPH ON LAP 52 • **RACE LEADERS:** HAMILTON 1-7; VETTEL 8-40; ROSBERG 41-52 •
* EXCLUDED FROM QUALIFYING FOR BEING UNDERWEIGHT • ** 10-PLACE GRID PENALTY FOR IGNORING BLUE FLAGS & FOR CHANGING GEARBOX

Lewis Hamilton suffered one of the many tyre blow-outs that were a feature of the race.

GERMAN GP

Sebastian Vettel had never won his home grand prix and he very nearly didn't last year, as Kimi Raikkonen's Lotus maintained better tyre life and the Finn closed in at the end and pushed him all the way to the finish line.

It was a case of another race and another pole for Lewis Hamilton and Mercedes. Again, however, the F1 W04's inability to make its tyres last in the midsummer heat at the Nurburgring meant that he fell back, finishing fifth.

Instead, the day belonged to Sebastian Vettel, who grabbed the lead when Hamilton was slow away, but it could have been different as Mark Webber edged in front but was squeezed out at the exit of Turn 1. They then ran in this order until their first tyre change on laps 7 and 8 respectively.

This left Romain Grosjean in the lead, and the fact that he was able to stay out until lap 13 showed how light his Lotus was on its tyres. While he continued to circulate, there was drama in the pits as Webber was waved away before his right wheel had been fitted and it came off, bounced down the pitlane and struck a cameraman. The Australian then had to be pulled back to have another wheel fitted and this dropped him to last.

Grosjean's long first run enabled him to jump Raikkonen and Hamilton as he rejoined second. He and Vettel were then assisted as Hamilton and Raikkonen were delayed by Jenson Button and Nico Hulkenberg, who had yet to stop. Raikkonen passed Hamilton at the chicane on lap 21 and then set off after Grosjean. The key to his attack was a long second stint and he kept going long after his team-mate and Vettel. He was still lapping fast and the team asked whether he could go to the finish on that set, but there was a radio problem that masked his answer and, erring on the side of caution, they called him in. Raikkonen duly came out 4s behind the lead duo, with Alonso coming out 4s behind him, and carved 0.5s off them each lap. Grosjean heeded instructions and let Raikkonen past on lap 55 and the Finn had five laps to catch his prey. The gap came down and he attacked into the chicane on the final lap but just wasn't close enough. Vettel, with his KERS working only intermittently, hung on.

Sebastian Vettel leads the Lotus duo and was made to work hard for his first home win.

NURBURGRING ROUND 9

DATE: **7 JULY 2013**

Laps: **60** • Distance: **191.769 miles/308.623km** • Weather: **Warm & sunny**

Pos	Driver	Team	Result	Stops	Qualifying Time	Grid
1	**Sebastian Vettel**	Red Bull	1h41m14.711s	3	1m29.501s	2
2	**Kimi Raikkonen**	Lotus	1h41m15.719s	3	1m29.892s	4
3	**Romain Grosjean**	Lotus	1h41m20.541s	3	1m29.959s	5
4	**Fernando Alonso**	Ferrari	1h41m22.432s	3	1m1.209s	8
5	**Lewis Hamilton**	Mercedes	1h41m41.638s	3	1m29.398s	1
6	**Jenson Button**	McLaren	1h41m42.707s	2	No time	9
7	**Mark Webber**	Red Bull	1h41m52.273s	3	1m29.608s	3
8	**Sergio Perez**	McLaren	1h41m53.017s	2	1m30.933s	13
9	**Nico Rosberg**	Mercedes	1h42m01.532s	3	1m30.326s	11
10	**Nico Hulkenberg**	Sauber	1h42m04.603s	3	No time	10
11	**Paul di Resta**	Force India	1h42m08.482s	2	1m30.697s	12
12	**Daniel Ricciardo**	Toro Rosso	1h42m11.686s	3	1m30.528s	6
13	**Adrian Sutil**	Force India	1h42m12.449s	3	1m31.010s	15
14	**Esteban Gutierrez**	Sauber	1h42m14.871s	3	1m31.010s	14
15	**Pastor Maldonado**	Williams	1h42m16.640s	2	1m31.707s	18
16	**Valtteri Bottas**	Williams	59 laps	2	1m31.693s	17
17	**Charles Pic**	Caterham	59 laps	3	1m32.937s	22*
18	**Giedo van der Garde**	Caterham	59 laps	3	1m33.734s	20
19	**Max Chilton**	Marussia	59 laps	4	1m34.098s	21
R	**Jean-Eric Vergne**	Toro Rosso	22 laps/hydraulics	1	1m31.104s	16
R	**Jules Bianchi**	Marussia	21 laps/engine	2	1m33.063s	19
R	**Felipe Massa**	Ferrari	3 laps/spun off	0	1m31.126s	7

FASTEST LAP: ALONSO, 1M33.468S, 123.205MPH/198.280KPH ON LAP 51 • RACE LEADERS: VETTEL 1-6, 14-40, 50-60; WEBBER 7-8; GROSJEAN 9-13; RAIKKONEN 41-49 • * 5-PLACE GRID PENALTY FOR GEARBOX CHANGE

HUNGARIAN GP

Nobody really anticipated a Mercedes win in Hungary, with 50-degree temperatures likely to hobble its cars by making their tyres degrade too fast. Yet Lewis Hamilton found his rubber lasted unexpectedly well and took his first win for the team.

Lewis Hamilton made it three poles in a row, although this surprised him as he hadn't thought that his lap was that special. Still, he said, qualifying was one thing and pace through the race another matter entirely.

So it was that he went into the race expecting his challengers from Red Bull and Lotus to beat him, judging by the superior pace they had shown on longer runs.

Hamilton led into Turn 1, with slow-starting Sebastian Vettel resisting Romain Grosjean's attempt to pass him around the outside. The Lotus driver then came under attack from Fernando Alonso at Turn 2, but held on. It all got hectic just behind the leaders and, three corners later, Nico Rosberg turned across Felipe Massa's front wing, damaging it.

It soon became clear that Hamilton's Mercedes wasn't losing pace, and he didn't pit until lap 9. Vettel came in on lap 11 and Grosjean two laps after that. What happened when they rejoined shaped the race, as all came out behind Jenson Button who was running a longer opening stint on the mediums. Hamilton blasted past the McLaren down the start/finish straight, but Vettel and Grosjean were stuck in his wake for 11 laps. By the time Vettel made it past, the gap between them had gone out from 1.7s pre-pitstop to 10s.

After Mark Webber rejoined from a long opening stint, he was caught by Button, who was still to pit, Vettel and Grosjean. A slip at Turn 5 let Vettel pass Button, who was then swamped, and Grosjean got past too but didn't leave him enough room at the chicane and this earned him a drivethrough penalty. Grosjean then passed Massa on the outside at Turn 4 and was penalized 20s for having had all his wheels beyond the white line.

Kimi Raikkonen had a quieter race in the other Lotus but by running a two-stop strategy advanced from fourth to second once the Red Bulls made their third stops. No one could stop Hamilton, though, who earned his first win for Mercedes.

HUNGARORING ROUND 10

DATE: **28 JULY 2013**

Laps: **70** • Distance: **190.531 miles/306.631km** • Weather: **Hot & sunny**

Pos	Driver	Team	Result	Stops	Qualifying Time	Grid
1	**Lewis Hamilton**	Mercedes	1h42m29.445s	3	1m19.388s	1
2	**Kimi Raikkonen**	Lotus	1h42m40.383s	2	1m19.851s	6
3	**Sebastian Vettel**	Red Bull	1h42m41.904s	3	1m19.426s	2
4	**Mark Webber**	Red Bull	1h42m47.489s	3	No time	10
5	**Fernando Alonso**	Ferrari	1h43m00.856s	3	1m19.791s	5
6	**Romain Grosjean**	Lotus	1h43m21.740s*	3	1m19.595s	3
7	**Jenson Button**	McLaren	1h43m23.264s	2	1m20.777s	13
8	**Felipe Massa**	Ferrari	1h43m25.892s	3	1m19.929s	7
9	**Sergio Perez**	McLaren	69 laps	2	1m22.398s	9
10	**Pastor Maldonado**	Williams	69 laps	3	1m21.133s	15
11	**Nico Hulkenberg**	Sauber	69 laps	2	1m20.580s	12
12	**Jean-Eric Vergne**	Toro Rosso	69 laps	3	1m21.029s	14
13	**Daniel Ricciardo**	Toro Rosso	69 laps	2	1m20.641s	8
14	**Giedo van der Garde**	Caterham	68 laps	3	1m23.333s	20
15	**Charles Pic**	Caterham	68 laps	2	1m23.007s	19
16	**Jules Bianchi**	Marussia	67 laps	3	1m23.787s	21
17	**Max Chilton**	Marussia	67 laps	3	1m23.997s	22
18	**Paul di Resta**	Force India	66 laps/hydraulics	3	1m22.043s	18
19	**Nico Rosberg**	Mercedes	64 laps/engine	3	1m19.720s	4
R	**Valtteri Bottas**	Williams	42 laps/hydraulics	2	1m21.219s	16
R	**Esteban Gutierrez**	Sauber	28 laps/gearbox	1	1m21.724s	17
R	**Adrian Sutil**	Force India	19 laps/hydraulics	0	1m20.569s	11

FASTEST LAP: WEBBER, 1M24.069S, 116.571MPH/1872.603KPH ON LAP 61 • **RACE LEADERS:** HAMILTON 1-8, 23-31, 35-50, 56-70; VETTEL 9-10, 32-34, 51-55; GROSJEAN 11-13; WEBBER 14-22 • * 20 SECOND PENALTY FOR CAUSING A COLLISION

Lewis Hamilton shows his delight at claiming his first win for Mercedes after a dominant drive.

BELGIAN GP

Lewis Hamilton's hopes of making it two wins in a row were extinguished early on the opening lap as Sebastian Vettel breezed past on the climb to Les Combes, and later he was demoted by Fernando Alonso and forced to settle for third place.

This race turned into another Sebastian Vettel/Red Bull tour de force, but few expected him to overpower pole man Lewis Hamilton so soon. Happy to sit in second place around La Source, he tucked under the Mercedes' rear wing as they accelerated down the hill. Vettel simply had more speed out of Raidillon and wafted past up the climb to Les Combes.

Vettel was then able to run at his own pace rather than, as had happened at previous races, sit bottled up behind one of the pole-starting Mercedes and be held up until they wore their tyres away.

But Fernando Alonso made the most progress early on, after qualifying only ninth after a spin. He not only gained four places by the exit of the first corner but then picked off Jenson Button and Nico Rosberg before the first of his two pitstops.

Hamilton had pitted already a couple of laps earlier, and then been delayed behind Romain Grosjean's yet-to-stop Lotus, which allowed Alonso to close in. Starting lap 14, the Spaniard made it through to second by passing the Mercedes into La Source. Once by, he had a clear run to second place, but there was nothing he could do about Vettel.

Hamilton was at least able to finish third, with Rosberg right behind him. Mark Webber was next home, again left to rue another poor start from which he found it hard to recover. At least he finished, though, which was more than Kimi Raikkonen managed - one the Finn's tear-off visor strips got lodged in a brake duct, causing them to overheat and his retirement.

The lap after he pulled off, Paul di Resta joined him on the sidelines, the victim of a move by Williams' Pastor Maldonado on Esteban Gutierrez at the Bus Stop that had him clip the other Force India of Adrian Sutil then veer across the Scot's path. Sergio Perez was also too robust and collected a drivethrough penalty for squeezing Grosjean off the track at Les Combes.

Lewis Hamilton leads into La Source but Sebastian Vettel didn't wait long before passing him.

SPA-FRANCORCHAMPS ROUND 11 — DATE: 7 JULY 2013

Laps: 44 • Distance: 191.419 miles/308.060km • Weather: Warm & sunny

Pos	Driver	Team	Result	Stops	Qualifying Time	Grid
1	Sebastian Vettel	Red Bull	1h23m42.196s	2	2m01.200s	2
2	Fernando Alonso	Ferrari	1h23m59.065s	2	2m03.482s	9
3	Lewis Hamilton	Mercedes	1h24m09.930s	2	2m01.012s	1
4	Nico Rosberg	Mercedes	1h24m12.068s	2	2m02.251s	4
5	Mark Webber	Red Bull	1h24m16.041s	2	2m01.325s	3
6	Jenson Button	McLaren	1h24m22.990s	2	2m03.075s	6
7	Felipe Massa	Ferrari	1h24m36.118s	2	2m04.059s	10
8	Romain Grosjean	Lotus	1h24m38.042s	1	2m03.081s	7
9	Adrian Sutil	Force India	1h24m51.743s	2	1m49.103s	12
10	Daniel Ricciardo	Toro Rosso	1h24m55.666s	2	2m03.317s	19
11	Sergio Perez	McLaren	1h25m04.132s	1	1m49.304s	13
12	Jean-Eric Vergne	Toro Rosso	1h25m08.936s	2	2m03.300s	18
13	Nico Hulkenberg	Sauber	1h25m10.454s	2	1m49.088s	11
14	Esteban Gutierrez	Sauber	1h25m22.632s	2	2m04.324s	21
15	Valtteri Bottas	Williams	1h25m29.652s	2	2m03.432s	20
16	Giedo van der Garde	Caterham	43 laps	2	1m52.036s	14
17	Pastor Maldonado	Williams	43 laps	2	2m03.072s	17
18	Jules Bianchi	Marussia	43 laps	2	1m52.563s	15
19	Max Chilton	Marussia	42 laps	2	1m52.762s	16
R	Paul di Resta	Force India	26 laps/accident	2	2m02.332s	5
R	Kimi Raikkonen	Lotus	25 laps/brakes	1	2m03.390s	8
R	Charles Pic	Caterham	8 laps/oil leak	0	2m07.384s	22

FASTEST LAP: VETTEL, 1M50.756S, 141.466MPH/227.668KPH ON LAP 40 • RACE LEADERS: VETTEL 1-44

ITALIAN GP

This was a gift to Sebastian Vettel as his rivals messed up qualifying and paid the price for that, leaving him to control the race from the front, with Nico Hulkenberg also starring as he raced his Sauber to fifth place.

Sebastian Vettel's hopes of maximum points at Monza received a boost when Lewis Hamilton ran wide, damaged the floor of his Mercedes and then got obstructed and so failed to get into the third qualifying session, ending his run of four poles in succession. When Kimi Raikkonen struggled as Lotus lost its speed in second qualifying, things looked better still for Vettel. Then, in the final reckoning, Ferrari messed up the timing of getting its cars onto the track at the right time to find space for their final qualifying runs, making the German think that his Christmas had come early. Indeed, with team-mate Mark Webber claiming the second grid slot and Nico Hulkenberg a quite remarkable third for Sauber ahead of the Ferraris of Felipe Massa and his closest championship rival Fernando Alonso, he could hardly stop smiling.

At the start, Webber made a better getaway for once, but then bogged down as he went through the gears, allowing Vettel to lead into the first chicane, followed by Massa after both Ferraris rocketed past Hulkenberg. Webber was third and Alonso fourth.

Raikkonen had made a fabulous start, but locked up and clouted Sergio Perez, sending the McLaren straight on and forcing the Finn to pit for a new nose, dropping him to last. After that, his speed was pace-setting, but his afternoon was all but futile. Still, he went further than Paul di Resta, who braked too late into the second chicane, hit Romain Grosjean and was out.

Vettel pulled clear, but it wasn't a smooth ride as he'd flatspotted a tyre braking into that first chicane and later had a gearbox problem, but he was never troubled. Alonso braved it around the outside of Webber at Roggia on lap 3, then Massa let him through to second, but he could do nothing about Vettel and had to settle for second, with Webber all over him. Massa came home fourth, with Hulkenberg doggedly resisting Rosberg for fifth. The Mercedes were the fastest on track,

MONZA ROUND 12

DATE: 28 JULY 2013

Laps: **53** • Distance: **190.587 miles/306.720km** • Weather: **Warm but overcast**

Pos	Driver	Team	Result	Stops	Qualifying Time	Grid
1	Sebastian Vettel	Red Bull	1h18m33.352s	1	1m23.755s	1
2	Fernando Alonso	Ferrari	1h18m38.819s	1	1m24.142s	5
3	Mark Webber	Red Bull	1h18m39.702s	1	1m23.968s	2
4	Felipe Massa	Ferrari	1h18m42.713s	1	1m24.132s	4
5	Nico Hulkenberg	Sauber	1h18m43.707s	1	1m24.065s	3
6	Nico Rosberg	Mercedes	1h18m44.351s	1	1m24.192s	6
7	Daniel Ricciardo	Toro Rosso	1h19m05.681s	1	1m24.209s	7
8	Romain Grosjean	Lotus	1h19m06.482s	1	1m24.848s	13
9	Lewis Hamilton	Mercedes	1h19m06.879s	2	1m24.803s	12
10	Jenson Button	McLaren	1h19m11.679s	1	1m24.515s	9
11	Kimi Raikkonen	Lotus	1h19m12.047s	2	1m24.610s	11
12	Sergio Perez	McLaren	1h19m13.117s	1	1m24.502s	8
13	Esteban Gutierrez	Sauber	1h19m14.232s	1	1m25.226s	16
14	Pastor Maldonado	Williams	1h19m22.437s	1	1m25.011s	14
15	Valtteri Bottas	Williams	1h19m30.179s	1	1m25.291s	18
16	Adrian Sutil	Force India	52 laps/brakes	1	1m24.932s	17*
17	Charles Pic	Caterham	52 laps	2	1m26.563s	20
18	Giedo van der Garde	Caterham	52 laps	2	1m26.406s	19
19	Jules Bianchi	Marussia	52 laps	1	1m27.085s	21
20	Max Chilton	Marussia	52 laps	1	1m27.480s	22
R	Jean-Eric Vergne	Toro Rosso	14 laps/transmission	0	1m28.050s	10
R	Paul di Resta	Force India	0 laps/accident	0	1m25.077s	15

FASTEST LAP: HAMILTON, 1M25.849S, 150.946MPH/242.924KPH ON LAP 51 • RACE LEADERS: VETTEL 1-23, 28-53; ALONSO 24-27 • * 3-PLACE GRID PENALTY FOR IMPEDING HAMILTON

Sebastian Vettel beams from top spot after his rivals made his race weekend straightforward.

but Rosberg lost ground when he missed a chicane, while an early puncture forced Hamilton to make an extra stop and his fightback took him only as far as ninth.

Vettel was booed on the podium by the tifosi, but having extended his points lead over Alonso to 53, he didn't appear to care too much.

SINGAPORE GP

The people booing Sebastian Vettel when he celebrated his victory on the podium brought the sport attention for all the wrong reasons. All the German had done was excel by making the most of his dominant Red Bull RB9 and doing what he's paid to do.

The Singapore GP looked simple for Vettel. He started on pole, led every lap, setting fastest lap, before stroking it to the finish line more than half a minute clear of Fernando Alonso's Ferrari, despite the field having been bunched up during the race by a safety car period. It was as complete a demolition of the field as could be imagined. Sure, the fans didn't like it, having wanted a closer race, but that was not his fault.

Alonso's second-place finish kept him in with an outside shot at the drivers' title, but the manner in which he'd been beaten left him in no doubt that this was merely a mathematical possibility. Yet again, though, the Spaniard had driven an exemplary race, which perhaps made his defeat all the harder to bear as he had leapt from seventh on the grid to third on the opening lap, demoting team-mate Felipe Massa, Lewis Hamilton, Mark Webber and Romain Grosjean.

Nico Rosberg had started on the front row, and even nosed his Mercedes ahead into the first corner, but Vettel wasn't having that and drove past him. He then simply escaped, and was 4s clear after just two laps. Rosberg continued in second until a slow second pitstop cost him time and position to Alonso, who had gambled on making his second stop just as a safety car came out on lap 25 after Daniel Ricciardo had crashed his Toro Rosso. This left Alonso to run a long final stint on mediums, but he did it.

Kimi Raikkonen made even more progress, as he rose from 13th on the grid, after his qualifying run was hampered by a back injury, to finish third.

It's not often that something memorable happens on the slowing down lap. However, when Webber went to hitch a lift home after his RB9's engine failed when fourth with a lap to go, he flagged down Alonso at Turn 7, then ignored marshals to run to the Ferrari and was adjudged to have done so in a dangerous manner. As this was his third reprimand of the year, he collected a 10-place grid penalty.

Hitching a ride back on Fernando Alonso's Ferrari wasn't the end of Mark Webber's problems.

MARINA BAY ROUND 13
DATE: 22 SEPTEMBER 2013

Laps: **61** • Distance: **191.906 miles/308.843km** • Weather: **Hot & humid**

Pos	Driver	Team	Result	Stops	Qualifying Time	Grid
1	Sebastian Vettel	Red Bull	1h59m13.132s	2	1m42.841.s	1
2	Fernando Alonso	Ferrari	1h59m45.759s	2	1m43.938s	7
3	Kimi Raikkonen	Lotus	1h59m57.052s	2	1m44.658s	13
4	Nico Rosberg	Mercedes	2h00m04.287s	2	1m42.932s	2
5	Lewis Hamilton	Mercedes	2h00m06.291s	2	1m43.254s	5
6	Felipe Massa	Ferrari	2h00m17.009s	3	1m43.890s	6
7	Jenson Button	McLaren	2h00m36.486s	2	1m44.282s	8
8	Sergio Perez	McLaren	2h00m36.952s	2	1m44.752s	14
9	Nico Hulkenberg	Sauber	2h00m37.393s	2	1m44.555s	11
10	Adrian Sutil	Force India	2h00m37.800s	3	1m45.185s	15
11	Pastor Maldonado	Williams	2h00m41.611s	3	1m46.619s	18
12	Esteban Gutierrez	Sauber	2h00m51.026s	2	No time	10
13	Valtteri Bottas	Williams	2h00m58.293s	3	1m45.388s	16
14	Jean-Eric Vergne	Toro Rosso	2h01m06.644s	3	1m44.588s	12
15	Mark Webber	Red Bull	60 laps/engine	2	1m43.152s	4
16	Giedo van der Garde	Caterham	60 laps	3	1m48.320s	20
17	Max Chilton	Marussia	60 laps	3	1m48.930s	22
18	Jules Bianchi	Marussia	60 laps	4	1m48.830s	21
19	Charles Pic	Caterham	60 laps	3	1m48.111s	19
20	Paul di Resta	Force India	54 laps/accident	2	1m46.121s	17
R	Romain Grosjean	Lotus	37 laps/engine	3	1m43.058s	3
R	Daniel Ricciardo	Toro Rosso	23 laps/accident	1	1m44.439s	9

FASTEST LAP: VETTEL, 1M48.574S, 104.358MPH/167.940KPH ON LAP 46 • RACE LEADERS: VETTEL 1-61

This was Sebastian Vettel's fourth win in succession. Yet, unlike in Singapore, he had company, as the Lotus duo were hot on his heels all the way to the finish, while Sauber's Nico Hulkenberg played a starring role by holding off Lewis Hamilton for fourth.

Sebastian Vettel was made to sweat for this victory. It came just a week after his runaway win in Singapore and was considerably harder for the German, but it left him on the brink of his fourth drivers' title. He led away from pole and was again never headed, but he had to nurse his right front tyre to ensure that he got to the finish in front.

This time, his main pursuer was Romain Grosjean, the Lotus driver enjoying a strong end-of-season run. The French driver had overtaken Lewis Hamilton's Mercedes on the first lap and tried to keep Vettel in sight.

There were two safety car periods and the first came on lap 31 when Sergio Perez's McLaren had lost the tread from its right front tyre at Turn 1. This allowed Grosjean to get right onto Vettel's tail. It also allowed Kimi Raikkonen onto his team-mate's tail, and Grosjean made a slight error into the second last corner after the safety car withdrew and Raikkonen passed him for second.

The safety car was soon back out after Adrian Sutil was over-ambitious when chasing Mark Webber's Red Bull and spun into it at Turn 3. The Australian's KERS then caught fire and the drivers were surprised to find that a fire tender had been deployed without permission from the FIA.

After everything was cleared up, with 14 laps still to run, racing got underway again and Vettel was able to creep clear, typically unable to go as slowly as the team requested to preserve his vulnerable front right tyre. The Lotus duo had no answer.

The best racing action was behind them as Nico Hulkenberg drove an exemplary race to keep the illustrious pair of Lewis Hamilton and Fernando Alonso behind him. The dicing was intense, but the Sauber driver never once put a wheel out of line. The Mercedes driver was left to rue having made a poor start that had let Grosjean get ahead of him, while team-mate Nico Rosberg did well to bounce back from a long stop while his front wing was replaced.

YEONGAM ROUND 14

DATE: **6 OCTOBER 2013**

Laps: **55** • Distance: **191.783 miles/308.645km** • Weather: **Hot & overcast**

Pos	Driver	Team	Result	Stops	Qualifying Time	Grid
1	Sebastian Vettel	Red Bull	1h43m13.701s	2	1m37.202s	1
2	Kimi Raikkonen	Lotus	1h43m17.925s	2	1m38.822s	9
3	Romain Grosjean	Lotus	1h43m18.628s	2	1m37.531s	3
4	Nico Hulkenberg	Sauber	1h43m37.815s	2	1m38.237s	7
5	Lewis Hamilton	Mercedes	1h43m38.956s	2	1m37.420s	2
6	Fernando Alonso	Ferrari	1h43m39.890s	2	1m38.038s	5
7	Nico Rosberg	Mercedes	1h43m40.399s	2	1m37.679s	4
8	Jenson Button	McLaren	1h43m45.963s	2	1m38.365s	11
9	Felipe Massa	Ferrari	1h43m48.091s	2	1m38.223s	6
10	Sergio Perez	McLaren	1h43m48.856s	2	1m38.362s	10
11	Esteban Gutierrez	Sauber	1h43m49.691s	2	1m38.405s	8
12	Valtteri Bottas	Williams	1h44m00.750s	2	1m39.470s	17
13	Pastor Maldonado	Williams	1h44m03.714s	2	1m39.987s	18
14	Charles Pic	Caterham	1h44m17.279s	2	1m40.864s	19
15	Giedo van der Garde	Caterham	1h44m18.202s	3	1m40.871s	20
16	Jules Bianchi	Marussia	1h44m21.671s	2	1m41.169s	22*
17	Max Chilton	Marussia	1h44m26.599s	2	1m41.322s	21
18	Jean-Eric Vergne	Toro Rosso	53 laps/brakes	3	1m38.781s	16
19	Daniel Ricciardo	Toro Rosso	52 laps/brakes	2	1m38.417s	12
20	Adrian Sutil	Force India	36 laps/collision	4	1m38.431s	14
R	Mark Webber	Red Bull	36 laps/accident damage	3	1m37.464s	13**
R	Paul di Resta	Force India	24 laps/spun off	2	1m38.718s	15

FASTEST LAP: VETTEL, 1M41.380S, 123.894MPH/199.388KPH ON LAP 53 • RACE LEADERS: VETTEL 1-55 • * 3-PLACE GRID PENALTY, ** 10-PLACE GRID PENALTY

Kimi Raikkonen moved ahead of Lotus team-mate Romain Grosjean to claim second place.

JAPANESE GP

Sebastian Vettel overcame a stern challenge from Romain Grosjean to claim his fifth win in a row, taking him to the brink of his fourth consecutive world crown, while ensuring that Red Bull Racing lifted the constructors' championship title.

The record books will show that this was Sebastian Vettel's ninth win of 2013, but it was far from routine – victory could easily have gone to his team-mate Mark Webber or Lotus racer Romain Grosjean.

Webber had hinted that this might be a meeting that didn't go the German's way when he out-qualified him for pole. In fact neither Red Bull led into the first corner as Grosjean rocketed past both from fourth on the grid. Lewis Hamilton, who'd started third, challenged briefly but was caught between the Red Bulls and his right rear tyre was clipped by Vettel and deflated, leading to an early retirement.

Webber's car carried less wing than the Lotus, so he couldn't get close enough to it through the last corner and therefore couldn't pass it down the main straight, allowing Grosjean to lead until he made the first of his two pitstops, on lap 12. This was a lap later than Webber, while Vettel waited until lap 14, but Grosjean continued in the lead. However, he was finally demoted when Vettel ran a longer second stint and came back out in front. By this point, Webber had been switched to a three-stop race, his chase of Grosjean in the first stint having eaten his medium tyres, but this tactic was to leave him seven seconds short after passing Grosjean with two laps to go.

Alonso, Raikkonen and the ever more impressive Hulkenberg completed the top half dozen, all more than half a minute behind Grosjean, with Esteban Gutierrez scoring his first points by finishing seventh in the second Sauber.

What was becoming increasingly clear at this point in the season was that the Renault V8 was the engine to have, with Mercedes making noises about how the unit used so successfully by Red Bull and Lotus might have advanced engine mapping settings and exhaust flow control to help wring out extra horsepower. For some, the 2014 season couldn't come soon enough.

112

Lotus racer Romain Grosjean takes the lead from Mark Webber and Lewis Hamilton into Turn 1.

SUZUKA ROUND 15

DATE: **13 OCTOBER 2013**

Laps: **53** • Distance: **191.224 miles/307.746km** • Weather: **Warm & sunny**

Pos	Driver	Team	Result	Stops	Qualifying Time	Grid
1	Sebastian Vettel	Red Bull	1h26m49.301s	2	1m31.089s	1
2	Mark Webber	Red Bull	1h26m56.430s	3	1m30.915s	2
3	Romain Grosjean	Lotus	1h26m59.211s	2	1m31.365s	4
4	Fernando Alonso	Ferrari	1h27m34.906s	2	1m31.665s	8
5	Kimi Raikkonen	Lotus	1h27m36.626s	2	1m31.684s	9
6	Nico Hulkenberg	Sauber	1h27m40.916s	2	1m31.644s	7
7	Esteban Gutierrez	Sauber	1h28m00.931s	2	1m32.063s	14
8	Nico Rosberg	Mercedes	1h28m01.324s	4	1m31.397s	6
9	Jenson Button	McLaren	1h28m10.122s	3	1m31.827s	10
10	Felipe Massa	Ferrari	1h28m18.564s	3	1m31.378s	5
11	Paul di Resta	Force India	1h28m27.873s	2	1m31.992s	12
12	Jean-Eric Vergne	Toro Rosso	52 laps	3	1m33.537s	17
13	Daniel Ricciardo	Toro Rosso	52 laps	3	1m32.485s	16
14	Adrian Sutil	Force India	52 laps	2	1m32.890s	22*
15	Sergio Perez	McLaren	52 laps	3	1m31.989s	11
16	Pastor Maldonado	Williams	52 laps	2	1m32.093s	15
17	Valtteri Bottas	Williams	52 laps	2	1m32.013s	13
18	Charles Pic	Caterham	52 laps	3	1m34.556s	20**
19	Max Chilton	Marussia	52 laps	2	1m34.320s	18
R	Lewis Hamilton	Mercedes	7 laps/collision	1	1m31.253s	3
R	Giedo van der Garde	Caterham	0 laps/collision	0	1m34.879s	19
R	Jules Bianchi	Marussia	0 laps/collision	0	1m34.958s	21**

FASTEST LAP: WEBBER, 1M34.587S, 137.332MPH/221.015KPH ON LAP 44 • RACE LEADERS: GROSJEAN 1-12, 15-28; VETTEL 13-14, 29-37, 43-53; WEBBER 38-42 • * 5-PLACE GRID PENALTY, ** 10-PLACE GRID PENALTY

INDIAN GP

Sebastian Vettel travelled to India knowing he could wrap up his fourth drivers' title, and he did so in the best possible way by winning the race as rival Fernando Alonso damaged his Ferrari in a first-lap clash and finished outside the points.

The Red Bull RB9 was in a class of its own around the swooping Buddh International Circuit, and Sebastian Vettel made the most of this to dictate how he ran his race. So confident was he of his car's pace that he pitted after just two laps to get rid of the soft tyres on which he started. This dropped him to 17th, but he was able to pick off car after car as he powered back up the order. Felipe Massa had assumed the lead when Vettel pitted, and stayed out until lap 8. By the time the Brazilian rejoined, though, Vettel was two places ahead of him. Two laps later, Vettel was a further two places to the good, up to fourth.

Team-mate Mark Webber had lost ground after he'd clashed with Kimi Raikkonen and Fernando Alonso at the first corner. This dropped him to seventh, but he advanced as Vettel, Nico Hulkenberg and Raikkonen pitted early. This was the stint in which Webber was supposed to sprint away in the lead as the drivers who'd started on softs called at the pits, and use the durability of his medium tyres to build a lead. He did get to the front, and stayed there until he pitted on lap 28. Vettel took over, but only for three laps before he was back in the pits again, changing to a second set of mediums. He lost the lead for only one lap, though, as Webber did just four laps on his softs before changing back to mediums. He was 12 seconds behind when he'd done this, but his secure second place turned to nothing when his alternator failed.

It was Nico Rosberg who claimed second place, half a minute down on his compatriot, with Romain Grosjean completing the most remarkable run from 17th on the grid to third thanks to a one-stop strategy and no little speed. Team-mate Raikkonen even had to be asked to get out of his way.

Famously, Vettel elected to risk the ire of the FIA by celebrating with some donuts, which sent the crowd wild and was as good a way as any to celebrate the crowning of an epic campaign.

BUDDH INT'L ROUND 16
DATE: 27 OCTOBER 2013
Laps: **60** • Distance: **190.925 miles/307.265km** • Weather: **Hot & overcast**

Pos	Driver	Team	Result	Stops	Qualifying Time	Grid
1	Sebastian Vettel	Red Bull	1h31m12.187s	2	1m24.119s	1
2	Nico Rosberg	Mercedes	1h31m42.010s	2	1m24.871s	2
3	Romain Grosjean	Lotus	1h31m52.079s	1	1m26.577s	17
4	Felipe Massa	Ferrari	1h31m53.879s	2	1m25.201s	5
5	Sergio Perez	McLaren	1h31m56.016s	2	1m26.153s	9
6	Lewis Hamilton	Mercedes	1h32m04.662s	2	1m24.941s	3
7	Kimi Raikkonen	Lotus	1h32m20.175s	2	1m25.248s	6
8	Paul di Resta	Force India	1h32m25.055s	2	1m25.711s	12
9	Adrian Sutil	Force India	1h32m26.921s	1	1m25.740s	13
10	Daniel Ricciardo	Toro Rosso	1h32m28.424s	2	1m25.519s	11
11	Fernando Alonso	Ferrari	1h32m30.484s	3	1m25.826s	8
12	Pastor Maldonado	Williams	1h32m31.138s	2	1m26.842s	18
13	Jean-Eric Vergne	Toro Rosso	59 laps	2	1m25.798s	14
14	Jenson Button	McLaren	59 laps	3	1m26.487s	10
15	Esteban Gutierrez	Sauber	59 laps	2	1m26.336s	16
16	Valtteri Bottas	Williams	59 laps	2	1m26.134s	15
17	Max Chilton	Marussia	58 laps	2	1m28.138s	22
18	Jules Bianchi	Marussia	58 laps	2	1m26.970s	19
19	Nico Hulkenberg	Sauber	54 laps/brakes	3	1m25.334s	7
R	Mark Webber	Red Bull	39 laps/alternator	2	1m25.047s	4
R	Charles Pic	Caterham	35 laps/hydraulics	2	1m27.487s	21
R	Giedo van der Garde	Caterham	1 lap/crash damage	0	1m27.105s	20

FASTEST LAP: RAIKKONEN, 1M27.679S, 130.753MPH/210.427KPH ON LAP 60 • **RACE LEADERS:** VETTEL 1-2, 29-31 & 33-60, MASSA 3-8, WEBBER 9-28 & 32

The FIA doesn't like them, but Sebastian Vettel performed some donuts to celebrate his title.

Winning his fourth drivers' title didn't slow Sebastian Vettel as he burst past team-mate Mark Webber off the grid and was never headed as he not only completed his seventh win in a row but did so by half a minute.

In Abu Dhabi, Vettel was once more effectively in a race of his own. He led every lap and was 30 seconds clear of Mark Webber after 55 laps. It was a complete victory.

Certainly, the Lotus attack wasn't as effective at Yas Marina, and neither was Mercedes', but the fact that the German ended up half a minute ahead of his own team-mate added emphasis to his superiority.

Away from the grid, it looked as though Webber had done enough to defend his pole position from an attack by Lewis Hamilton's fast-starting Mercedes, but as he did so Vettel simply drove around the outside of both, with Nico Rosberg following after him in the other Mercedes. Hamilton ended up fifth by the exit of the corner as Romain Grosjean slotted into fourth, and he was to spend the race struggling for grip.

Kimi Raikkonen had been in the news when he failed to show for media commitments on the Thursday, saying that as the team hadn't paid him his wages all season, he was no longer doing any. His race was almost as short, as he hit the left rear tyre of Giedo van der Garde's Caterham and damaged his suspension. Jenson Button was in the wars on the opening lap for the second race in a row, and having his car's nose changed wrecked his race.

For once, Webber's luck didn't desert him and he was able to overtake Rosberg on lap 20 and race to second place, albeit far behind Vettel. The order behind was fairly static, with Grosjean finishing on Rosberg's tail, before a gap of more than half a minute back to Fernando Alonso, who passed Paul di Resta's Force India for fifth a few laps from the end, something that Hamilton just failed to do.

Knowing that he had become all but untouchable, Vettel entertained the fans to more donuts on his slowing down lap, then drove to parc ferme as the rules insist.

Nico Rosberg put his Mercedes between the Red Bulls but later had to settle for third place.

YAS MARINA ROUND 17

DATE: **3 NOVEMBER 2013**

Laps: **55** • Distance: **189.738 miles/305.355km** • Weather: **Hot & sunny**

Pos	Driver	Team	Result	Stops	Qualifying Time	Grid
1	Sebastian Vettel	Red Bull	1h38m06.106s	2	1m40.075s	2
2	Mark Webber	Red Bull	1h38m36.935s	2	1m39.957s	1
3	Nico Rosberg	Mercedes	1h38m39.756s	2	1m40.419s	3
4	Romain Grosjean	Lotus	1h38m40.908s	2	1m40.997s	6
5	Fernando Alonso	Ferrari	1h39m13.287s	2	1m41.093s	10
6	Paul di Resta	Force India	1h39m24.280s	1	1m41.133s	11
7	Lewis Hamilton	Mercedes	1h39m25.373s	2	1m40.501s	4
8	Felipe Massa	Ferrari	1h39m28.992s	2	1m41.015s	7
9	Sergio Perez	McLaren	1h39m37.304s	2	1mx41.068s	8
10	Adrian Sutil	Force India	1h39m39.363s	1	1m42.051s	17
11	Pastor Maldonado	Williams	1h39m42.095s	2	1m41.395s	14
12	Jenson Button	McLaren	1h39m49.873s	2	1m41.200s	12
13	Esteban Gutierrez	Sauber	1h39m50.401s	2	1m41.999s	16
14	Nico Hulkenberg	Sauber	54 laps	3	1m40.576s	5
15	Valtteri Bottas	Williams	54 laps	2	1m41.447s	15
16	Daniel Ricciardo	Toro Rosso	54 laps	2	1m41.111s	9
17	Jean-Eric Vergne	Toro Rosso	54 laps	2	1m41.279s	13
18	Giedo van der Garde	Caterham	54 laps	2	1m43.252s	18
19	Charles Pic	Caterham	54 laps	2	1m43.528s	19
20	Jules Bianchi	Marussia	53 laps	2	1m43.398s	21*
21	Max Chilton	Marussia	53 laps	2	1m44.198s	20
R	Kimi Raikkonen	Lotus	0 laps/accident	0	No time	22^

FASTEST LAP: ALONSO, 1M43.434S, 120.114MPH/193.305KPH ON LAP 55 • RACE LEADERS: VETTEL 1-55 • * 5-PLACE GRID PENALTY, ^ EXCLUDED FROM QUALIFYING FOR A TECHNICAL INFRINGEMENT

UNITED STATES GP

Sebastian Vettel's victory in Austin made him the first driver to win eight grands prix consecutively in a single season, with his rivals unable to do anything about his pace. Romain Grosjean was best of the rest, ahead of Mark Webber.

The drivers' second visit to the Circuit of the Americas was a treat, because it's by far the best new circuit of recent years, offering spectacular backdrops and dynamic corners. Trouble is, come the race, no one could prevent Sebastian Vettel from continuing his run of wins that started at the German GP in July. He controlled the race from the front and by making it eight wins in a row in a single season, he set a record.

Webber was not only unable to pass Vettel for the lead at the start, but found himself pinched on the inside line, and both Romain Grosjean and Lewis Hamilton passed him around the outside. Webber then closed in on the Mercedes and demoted it with an aggressive move into Turn 12 on lap 13. He then spent the rest of the race jousting for position with Romain Grosjean, but the ever-improving French driver refused to crack and so kept the position.

Hamilton was in a testy mood on his race radio, wanting less, then more, information from the pitwall as the race wore on. Either way, fourth place was his best result for seven rounds. Team-mate Nico Rosberg had qualified only 14th and could climb no higher than ninth.

Ferrari were also slightly at sea in Texas, but Fernando Alonso started sixth and finished there too. McLaren meanwhile had the awkward outcome of the driver they had just released for 2014, Sergio Perez, comprehensively beating the one they would be keeping on, Jenson Button, the Mexican and the British driver classified seventh and 10th respectively.

With Kimi Raikkonen quitting Lotus to have back surgery (against the backdrop of having not being paid all year) fellow Finn Heikki Kovalainen filled his seat and showed flashes of speed to get through to the final qualifying session. In the race, however, he was swamped at the start and later suffered front wing damage and KERS failure that dropped him from eighth to 14th.

AUSTIN ROUND 18

DATE: **17 NOVEMBER 2013**

Laps: **56** • Distance: **191.912 miles/308.853km** • Weather: **Hot & sunny**

Pos	Driver	Team	Result	Stops	Qualifying Time	Grid
1	Sebastian Vettel	Red Bull	1h39m17.148s	1	1m36.338s	1
2	Romain Grosjean	Lotus	1h39m23.432s	1	1m37.155s	3
3	Mark Webber	Red Bull	1h39m35.544s	1	1m36.441s	2
4	Lewis Hamilton	Mercedes	1h39m44.506s	1	1m37.345s	5
5	Fernando Alonso	Ferrari	1h39m46.740s	1	1m37.376s	6
6	Nico Hulkenberg	Sauber	1h39m47.548s	1	1m37.296s	4
7	Sergio Perez	McLaren	1h40m03.840s	1	1m37.452s	7
8	Valtteri Bottas	Williams	1h40m11.657s	1	1m37.836s	9
9	Nico Rosberg	Mercedes	1h40m16.289s	1	1m38.364s	12
10	Jenson Button	McLaren	1h40m34.426s	1	1m38.217s	15*
11	Daniel Ricciardo	Toro Rosso	1h40m38.152s	1	1m38.131s	10
12	Felipe Massa	Ferrari	1h40m44.062s	2	1m38.592s	13
13	Esteban Gutierrez	Sauber	1h40m48.855s	2	1m38.034s	20^
14	Heikki Kovalainen	Lotus	1h40m52.211s	2	1m37.715s	8
15	Paul di Resta	Force India	1h40m54.001s	2	1m38.139s	11
16	Jean-Eric Vergne	Toro Rosso	1h41m01.722s^^	1	1m38.6969s	14
17	Pastor Maldonado	Williams	55 laps	1	1m39.351s	17
18	Jules Bianchi	Marussia	55 laps	1	1m40.528s	19
19	Giedo van der Garde	Caterham	55 laps	1	1m40.491s	18
20	Charles Pic	Caterham	55 laps	2	1m40.596s	22**
21	Max Chilton	Marussia	54 laps	2	1m41.401s	21
R	Adrian Sutil	Force India	0 laps/accident	0	1m39.250s	16

FASTEST LAP: VETTEL, 1M39.856S, 123.500MPH/198.754KPH ON LAP 54 • RACE LEADERS: VETTEL 1-27, 30-56, GROSJEAN 28-29 • * 3-PLACE GRID PENALTY, ** 5-PLACE GRID PENALTY, ^ 10-PLACE GRID PENALTY, ^^ 20-SECOND PENALTY FOR COLLIDING WITH GUTIERREZ

Romain Grosjean was pushed all the way by Mark Webber but held on for second place.

BRAZILIAN GP

Having claimed pole by a wide margin, Sebastian Vettel recovered from being beaten to the first corner to sweep ahead at the end of the opening lap, never to be headed again, and so achieve a record ninth win in a row.

Meteorologists forecast rain for the Brazilian GP and it certainly added spice to proceedings and some spectacle for the fans as the drivers scrambled in qualifying. Almost inevitably, just to depress his rivals yet further, Sebastian Vettel not only claimed pole but did so by a whopping 0.623s ahead of Nico Rosberg, with Fernando Alonso just deprived of his first front row position of the year and his own team-mate Mark Webber fourth.

At the start, the fans were wildly excited when Rosberg nosed his Silver Arrow ahead on the sprint to the first corner, then held his line into this dropping lefthander and kept the position as the field followed him down the dip. Was Vettel going to have to fight for this one? Not for long, as the Red Bull driver closed in and found the grip out of the final corner to accelerate early enough to slingshot past.

After that there was just one small scare for Vettel, when his pitcrew just got its call through to him to pit before he passed the pit entry as the safety car was deployed on lap 46 after Valtteri Bottas and Lewis Hamilton clashed, leaving the Williams marooned trackside. At this very moment, the Red Bull mechanics were waiting with Webber's new set of tyres, so had to put these down, find Vettel's, make Vettel's pitstop and then follow up with one for Webber, who had been waiting behind him.

Somehow, they got away with this confusion and not only did Vettel resume in the lead, but Webber came out still second, and so Alonso, who pitted at the same time, stayed third. Felipe Massa might have finished fourth on his final Ferrari outing, and Alonso said later that he'd have let him past for third but he, like Hamilton, was hit by a drivethrough penalty, his for cutting across the pit entry line. This cost the Brazilian time and he would finish seventh.

Fourth place went instead to McLaren, with Jenson Button giving the team its best finish of an awful season.

Sebastian Vettel waves to the crowd in acknowledgement of a brilliant fourth drivers' title.

INTERLAGOS ROUND 19

DATE: **23 NOVEMBER 2013**

Laps: **71** • Distance: **190.067 miles/305.884km** • Weather: **Overcast then light rain**

Pos	Driver	Team	Result	Stops	Qualifying Time	Grid
1	Sebastian Vettel	Red Bull	1h32m36.300s	2	1m26.479s	1
2	Mark Webber	Red Bull	1h32m46.752s	2	1m27.572s	4
3	Fernando Alonso	Ferrari	1h32m55.213s	2	1m27.539s	3
4	Jenson Button	McLaren	1h33m13.660s	2	1m28.308s	14
5	Nico Rosberg	Mercedes	1h33m15.348s	2	1m27.102s	2
6	Sergio Perez	McLaren	1h33m20.351s	2	1m28.269s	19*
7	Felipe Massa	Ferrari	1h33m25.410s	3	1m28.109s	9
8	Nico Hulkenberg	Sauber	1h33m40.552s	2	1m29.582s	10
9	Lewis Hamilton	Mercedes	1h33m49.203s	3	1m27.677s	5
10	Daniel Ricciardo	Toro Rosso	70 laps	2	1m28.052s	7
11	Paul di Resta	Force India	70 laps	2	1m27.798s	12
12	Esteban Gutierrez	Sauber	70 laps	2	1m27.445s	17
13	Adrian Sutil	Force India	70 laps	3	1m28.586s	15
14	Heikki Kovalainen	Lotus	70 laps	2	1m27.456s	11
15	Jean-Eric Vergne	Toro Rosso	70 laps	3	1m28.081s	8
16	Pastor Maldonado	Williams	70 laps	2	1m27.367s	16
17	Jules Bianchi	Marussia	69 laps	2	1m28.366s	21
18	Giedo van der Garde	Caterham	69 laps	3	1m28.320s	20
19	Max Chilton	Marussia	69 laps	3	1m28.950s	22
R	Charles Pic	Caterham	58 laps/suspension	1	1m27.843s	18
R	Valtteri Bottas	Williams	45 laps/collision	2	1m27.954s	13
R	Romain Grosjean	Lotus	2 laps/engine	0	1m27.737s	6

FASTEST LAP: WEBBER, 1M15.436S, 127.776MPH/205.636KPH ON LAP 51 • RACE LEADERS: VETTEL 1-71 • * 5-PLACE GRID PENALTY

A helmet-less Mark Webber takes a lap of honour at the end of the 2013 Brazilian GP, bringing to a close his highly successful – and highly respected – Formula One career.

POS	DRIVER	NAT		CAR-ENGINE	R1	R2	R3	R4	R5
1	SEBASTIAN VETTEL	GER		RED BULL-RENAULT RB9	3P	1P	4F	1F	4
2	FERNANDO ALONSO	SPA		FERRARI F138	2	R	1	8	1
3	MARK WEBBER	AUS		RED BULL-RENAULT RB9	6	2	R	7	5
4	LEWIS HAMILTON	GBR		MERCEDES F1 W04	5	3	3P	5	12
5	KIMI RAIKKONEN	FIN		LOTUS-RENAULT E21	1F	7	2	2	2
6	NICO ROSBERG	GER		MERCEDES F1 W04	R	4	R	9P	6P
7	ROMAIN GROSJEAN	FRA		LOTUS-RENAULT E21	10	6	9	3	R
8	FELIPE MASSA	BRA		FERRARI F138	4	5	6	15	3
9	JENSON BUTTON	GBR		McLAREN-MERCEDES MP4-28	9	17	5	10	8
10	NICO HULKENBERG	GER		SAUBER-FERRARI C32	NS	8	10	12	15
11	SERGIO PEREZ	MEX		McLAREN-MERCEDES MP4-28	11	9F	11	6	9
12	PAUL DI RESTA	GBR		FORCE INDIA-MERCEDES VJM06	8	R	8	4	7
13	ADRIAN SUTIL	GER		FORCE INDIA-MERCEDES VJM06	7	R	R	13	13
14	DANIEL RICCIARDO	AUS		TORO ROSSO-FERRARI STR8	R	18	7	16	10
15	JEAN-ERIC VERGNE	FRA		TORO ROSSO-FERRARI STR8	12	10	12	R	R
16	ESTEBAN GUTIERREZ	MEX		SAUBER-FERRARI C32	13	12	R	18	11F
17	VALTTERI BOTTAS	FIN		WILLIAMS-RENAULT FW35	14	11	13	14	16
18	PASTOR MALDONADO	VEN		WILLIAMS-RENAULT FW35	R	R	14	11	14
19	JULES BIANCHI	FRA		MARUSSIA-COSWORTH MR-02	15	13	15	19	18
20	CHARLES PIC	FRA		CATERHAM-RENAULT CT03	16	14	16	17	17
21	GIEDO VAN DER GARDE	NED		CATERHAM-RENAULT CT03	18	15	18	21	R
22	MAX CHILTON	GBR		MARUSSIA-COSWORTH MR-02	17	16	17	20	19
23	HEIKKI KOVALAINEN	FIN		LOTUS-RENAULT E21	-	-	-	-	-

SCORING

1st	25 points
2nd	18 points
3rd	15 points
4th	12 points
5th	10 points
6th	8 points
7th	6 points
8th	4 points
9th	2 points
10th	1 point

	R1	R2	R3	R4	R5
RED BULL-RENAULT	3/6	1/2	4/R	1/7	4/5
MERCEDES	5/R	3/4	3/R	5/9	6/12
FERRARI	2/4	5/R	1/6	8/15	1/3
LOTUS-RENAULT	1/10	6/7	2/9	2/3	2/R
McLAREN-MERCEDES	9/11	9/17	5/11	6/10	8/9
FORCE INDIA-MERCEDES	7/8	R/R	8/R	4/13	7/13
SAUBER-FERRARI	13/NS	8/12	10/R	12/18	11/15
TORO ROSSO-FERRARI	12/R	10/18	7/12	16/R	10/R
WILLIAMS-RENAULT	14/R	11/R	13/14	11/14	14/16
MARUSSIA-COSWORTH	15/17	13/16	15/17	19/20	18/19
CATERHAM-RENAULT	16/18	14/15	16/18	17/21	17/R

SYMBOLS AND GRAND PRIX KEY

ROUND 1 ....AUSTRALIAN GP	ROUND 6 ....MONACO GP	ROUND 11...................BELGIAN GP	ROUND 16 ....INDIAN GP
ROUND 2 ....MALAYSIAN GP	ROUND 7....................CANADIAN GP	ROUND 12......................ITALIAN GP	ROUND 17......................ABU DHABI GP
ROUND 3 ....CHINESE GP	ROUND 8.......................BRITISH GP	ROUND 13.............SINGAPORE GP	ROUND 18 ....UNITED STATES GP
ROUND 4 ....BAHRAIN GP	ROUND 9.....................GERMAN GP	ROUND 14 ....KOREAN GP	ROUND 19 ....BRAZILIAN GP
ROUND 5 ....SPANISH GP	ROUND 10 ....HUNGARIAN GP	ROUND 15..............JAPANESE GP	

D DISQUALIFIED   **F** FASTEST LAP   **NC** NOT CLASSIFIED   **NS** NON-STARTER   **P** POLE POSITION   **R** RETIRED   **W** WITHDRAWN

R6	R7	R8	R9	R10	R11	R12	R13	R14	R15	R16	R17	R18	R19	TOTAL
2F	1P	R	1	3	1F	1P	1PF	1PF	1	1P	1	1PF	1P	397
7	2	3	4F	5	2	2	2	6	4	11	5F	5	3	242
3	4F	2F	7	4F	5	3	15	R	2PF	R	2P	3	2F	199
4	3	4P	5P	1P	3P	9F	5	5	R	6	7	4	9	189
10	9	5	2	2	R	11	3	2	5	7F	R	-	-	183
1P	5	1	9	19	4	6	4	7	8	2	3	9	5	171
R	13	19	3	6	8	8	R	3	3	3	4	2	R	132
R	8	6	R	8	7	4	6	9	10	4	8	12	7	112
6	12	13	6	7	6	10	7	8	9	14	12	10	4	73
11	R	10	10	11	13	5	9	4	6	11	14	6	8	51
16	11	20	8	9	11	12	8	10	15	5	9	7	6	49
9	7	9	11	18	R	R	20	R	11	8	6	15	11	48
5	10	7	13	R	9	16	10	R	14	9	10	R	13	29
R	15	8	12	13	10	7	R	R	13	10	16	11	10	20
8	6	R	R	12	12	R	14	R	12	13	17	16	15	13
13	20	14	14	R	14	13	12	11	7	15	13	13	12	6
12	14	12	16	R	15	15	13	12	17	16	15	8	R	4
R	16	11	15	10	17	14	11	13	16	12	11	17	16	1
R	17	16	R	16	18	19	18	16	R	18	20	18	17	
R	18	15	17	15	R	17	19	14	18	R	19	20	R	
15	R	18	18	14	16	18	16	15	R	R	18	19	18	
14	19	17	19	17	19	20	17	17	19	17	21	21	19	
-	-	-	-	-	-	-	-	-	-	-	-	14	14	

119

2/3	1/4	2/R	1/7	3/4	1/5	1/3	1/15	1/R	1/2	1/R	1/2	1/3	1/2	596
1/4	3/5	1/4	5/9	1/19	3/4	6/9	4/5	5/7	8/R	2/6	3/7	4/9	5/9	360
7/R	2/8	3/6	4/R	5/8	2/7	2/4	2/6	6/9	4/10	4/11	5/8	5/12	3/7	354
10/R	9/13	15/19	2/3	2/6	8/R	8/11	3/R	2/3	3/5	3/7	4/R	2/14	14/R	315
6/16	11/12	13/20	6/8	7/9	6/11	10/12	7/8	8/10	9/15	5/14	9/12	7/10	4/6	122
5/9	7/10	7/9	11/13	18/R	9/R	16/R	10/20	R/R	11/14	8/9	6/10	15/R	11/13	77
11/13	20/R	10/14	10/14	11/R	13/14	5/13	9/12	4/11	6/7	11/15	13/14	6/13	8/12	57
8/R	6/15	8/R	12/R	12/13	10/12	7/R	14/R	R/R	12/13	10/13	16/17	11/16	10/15	33
12/R	14/16	11/12	15/16	10/R	15/17	14/15	11/13	12/13	16/17	12/16	11/15	8/17	16/R	5
14/R	17/19	16/17	19/R	16/17	18/19	19/20	17/18	16/17	19/R	17/18	20/21	18/21	17/19	
15/R	18/R	15/18	17/18	14/15	16/R	17/18	16/19	14/15	18/R	R/R	18/19	19/20	18/R	

FORMULA ONE RECORDS

MOST STARTS

DRIVERS

325	Rubens Barrichello	(BRA)	161	Ayrton Senna	(BRA)
308	Michael Schumacher	(GER)	159	Heinz-Harald Frentzen	(GER)
256	Riccardo Patrese	(ITA)	158	Martin Brundle	(GBR)
	Jarno Trulli	(ITA)		Olivier Panis	(FRA)
247	Jenson Button	(GBR)	152	John Watson	(GBR)
	David Coulthard	(GBR)	149	Rene Arnoux	(FRA)
230	Giancarlo Fisichella	(ITA)	147	Eddie Irvine	(GBR)
217	Fernando Alonso	(SPA)		Nico Rosberg	(FIN)
216	Mark Webber	(AUS)		Derek Warwick	(GBR)
210	Gerhard Berger	(AUT)	146	Carlos Reutemann	(ARG)
208	Andrea de Cesaris	(ITA)	144	Emerson Fittipaldi	(BRA)
204	Nelson Piquet	(BRA)	135	Jean-Pierre Jarier	(FRA)
201	Jean Alesi	(FRA)	132	Eddie Cheever	(USA)
199	Alain Prost	(FRA)		Clay Regazzoni	(SWI)
194	Michele Alboreto	(ITA)	129	Lewis Hamilton	(GBR)
	Kimi Raikkonen	(FIN)	128	Mario Andretti	(USA)
192	Felipe Massa	(BRA)	126	Jack Brabham	(AUS)
187	Nigel Mansell	(GBR)	123	Ronnie Peterson	(SWE)
185	Nick Heidfeld	(GER)	120	Sebastian Vettel	(GER)
180	Ralf Schumacher	(GER)	119	Pierluigi Martini	(ITA)
176	Graham Hill	(GBR)	116	Damon Hill	(GBR)
175	Jacques Laffite	(FRA)		Jacky Ickx	(BEL)
171	Niki Lauda	(AUT)		Alan Jones	(AUS)
165	Jacques Villeneuve	(CDN)	114	Keke Rosberg	(FIN)
163	Thierry Boutsen	(BEL)		Patrick Tambay	(FRA)
162	Mika Hakkinen	(FIN)	112	Denny Hulme	(NZL)
	Johnny Herbert	(GBR)		Jody Scheckter	(RSA)

CONSTRUCTORS

870	Ferrari
743	McLaren
662	Williams
534	Lotus* (nee Toleman, then Benetton, then Renault II)
492	Lotus
488	Toro Rosso (nee Minardi)
418	Tyrrell
409	Prost (nee Ligier)
397	Force India (nee Jordan, then Midland, then Spyker)
394	Brabham
383	Arrows
364	Sauber (including BMW Sauber)
301	Renault
300	Red Bull (nee Stewart, then Jaguar Racing)
230	March
227	Mercedes GP (nee BAR, then Honda Racing, then Brawn GP)
197	BRM
132	Osella

* See key on page 125 for explanation of how figures are attributed to teams that have changed their names since they started in F1.

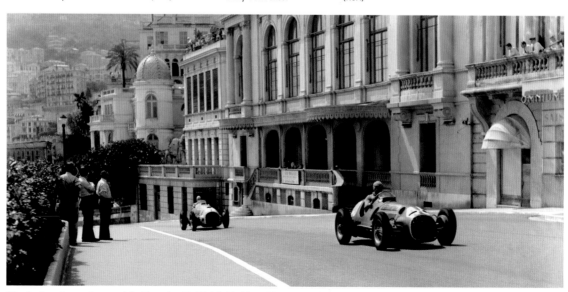

Alberto Ascari races to second for Ferrari on his F1 debut in the 1950 Monaco GP, taking a bold step in a career that would land him two titles.

Alain Prost guides his Williams FW15C towards his then record-extending 51st and final grand prix win in the 1993 German GP at Hockenheim.

MOST WINS

DRIVERS

91	Michael Schumacher	(GER)	16	Stirling Moss	(GBR)	Ronnie Peterson	(SWE)
51	Alain Prost	(FRA)	15	Jenson Button	(GBR)	Jody Scheckter	(RSA)
41	Ayrton Senna	(BRA)	14	Jack Brabham	(AUS)	9	Mark Webber	(AUS)
39	Sebastian Vettel	(GER)		Emerson Fittipaldi	(BRA)	8	Denny Hulme	(NZL)
32	Fernando Alonso	(SPA)		Graham Hill	(GBR)		Jacky Ickx	(BEL)
31	Nigel Mansell	(GBR)	13	Alberto Ascari	(ITA)	7	Rene Arnoux	(FRA)
27	Jackie Stewart	(GBR)		David Coulthard	(GBR)		Juan Pablo Montoya	(COL)
25	Jim Clark	(GBR)	12	Mario Andretti	(USA)	6	Tony Brooks	(GBR)
	Niki Lauda	(AUT)		Alan Jones	(AUS)		Jacques Laffite	(FRA)
24	Juan Manuel Fangio	(ARG)		Carlos Reutemann	(ARG)		Riccardo Patrese	(ITA)
23	Nelson Piquet	(BRA)	11	Rubens Barrichello	(BRA)		Jochen Rindt	(AUT)
22	Lewis Hamilton	(GBR)		Felipe Massa	(BRA)		Ralf Schumacher	(GER)
	Damon Hill	(GBR)		Jacques Villeneuve	(CDN)		John Surtees	(GBR)
20	Mika Hakkinen	(FIN)	10	Gerhard Berger	(AUT)		Gilles Villeneuve	(CDN)
	Kimi Raikkonen	(FIN)		James Hunt	(GBR)			

CONSTRUCTORS

221	Ferrari	15	Renault		Wolf
181	McLaren	13	Mercedes GP (including Honda	2	Honda
114	Williams		Racing, Brawn GP)	1	BMW Sauber
79	Lotus	10	Alfa Romeo		Eagle
49	Lotus* (including Benetton,	9	Ligier		Hesketh
	Renault II)		Maserati		Penske
48	Red Bull (including Stewart)		Matra		Porsche
35	Brabham		Mercedes		Shadow
23	Tyrrell		Vanwall		Stewart
17	BRM	4	Jordan		Toro Rosso
16	Cooper	3	March		

MOST WINS IN ONE SEASON

Jim Clark gets his 1965 season going by winning the South African GP in East London, this being the first of six victories in the first six races.

DRIVERS

13	Michael Schumacher	2004		Ayrton Senna	1988	Alberto Ascari	1952
	Sebastian Vettel	2013	**7**	Fernando Alonso	2005	Jim Clark	1965
11	Michael Schumacher	2002		Fernando Alonso	2006	Juan Manuel Fangio	1954
	Sebastian Vettel	2011		Jim Clark	1963	Damon Hill	1994
9	Nigel Mansell	1992		Alain Prost	1984	James Hunt	1976
	Michael Schumacher	1995		Alain Prost	1988	Nigel Mansell	1987
	Michael Schumacher	2000		Alain Prost	1993	Kimi Raikkonen	2007
	Michael Schumacher	2001		Kimi Raikkonen	2005	Michael Schumacher	1998
8	Mika Hakkinen	1998		Ayrton Senna	1991	Michael Schumacher	2003
	Damon Hill	1996		Jacques Villeneuve	1997	Michael Schumacher	2006
	Michael Schumacher	1994	**6**	Mario Andretti	1978	Ayrton Senna	1989 & 1990

CONSTRUCTORS

15	Ferrari	2002		Ferrari	2006	Williams	1997
	Ferrari	2004		Ferrari	2007	**7** Ferrari	1952
	McLaren	1988		McLaren	1998	Ferrari	1953
13	Red Bull	2013		Red Bull	2010	Ferrari	2008
12	McLaren	1984		Williams	1986	Lotus	1963
	Red Bull	2011		Williams	1987	Lotus	1973
	Williams	1996	**8**	Benetton	1994	McLaren	1999
11	Benetton	1995		Brawn GP	2009	McLaren	2000
10	Ferrari	2000		Ferrari	2003	McLaren	2012
	McLaren	2005		Lotus	1978	Red Bull	2012
	McLaren	1989		McLaren	1991	Tyrrell	1971
	Williams	1992		McLaren	2007	Williams	1991
	Williams	1993		Renault	2005	Williams	1994
9	Ferrari	2001		Renault	2006		

MOST POLE POSITIONS

DRIVERS

68	Michael Schumacher	(GER)
65	Ayrton Senna	(BRA)
45	Sebastian Vettel	(GER)
33	Jim Clark	(GBR)
	Alain Prost	(FRA)
32	Nigel Mansell	(GBR)
31	Lewis Hamilton	(GBR)
29	Juan Manuel Fangio	(ARG)
26	Mika Hakkinen	(FIN)
24	Niki Lauda	(AUT)
	Nelson Piquet	(BRA)
22	Fernando Alonso	(SPA)
20	Damon Hill	(GBR)
18	Mario Andretti	(USA)
	Rene Arnoux	(FRA)
17	Jackie Stewart	(GBR)

16	Stirling Moss	(GBR)
	Kimi Raikkonen	(FIN)
15	Felipe Massa	(BRA)
14	Alberto Ascari	(ITA)
	Rubens Barrichello	(BRA)
	James Hunt	(GBR)
	Ronnie Peterson	(SWE)
13	Jack Brabham	(AUS)
	Graham Hill	(GBR)
	Jacky Ickx	(BEL)
	Juan Pablo Montoya	(COL)
	Jacques Villeneuve	(CDN)
	Mark Webber	(AUS)
12	Gerhard Berger	(AUT)
	David Coulthard	(GBR)
10	Jochen Rindt	(AUT)

CONSTRUCTORS

207	Ferrari
154	McLaren
127	Williams
107	Lotus
58	Red Bull
39	Brabham
34	Lotus* (including Toleman, Benetton, Renault II)
31	Renault
17	Mercedes GP (including BAR, Honda Raing, Brawn GP)
14	Tyrrell
12	Alfa Romeo
11	BRM
	Cooper
10	Maserati
9	Ligier
8	Mercedes
7	Vanwall
5	March
4	Matra
3	Force India (including Jordan)
	Shadow
	Toyota
2	Lancia
1	BMW Sauber
	Toro Rosso

Ayrton Senna made his first pole position count by going on to score his first F1 win in the 1985 Portuguese GP for Lotus at a wet Estoril.

FASTEST LAPS

DRIVERS

76	Michael Schumacher	(GER)		Mark Webber	(AUS)	228	Ferrari	
41	Alain Prost	(FRA)	18	David Coulthard	(GBR)	152	McLaren	
39	Kimi Raikkonen	(FIN)	17	Rubens Barrichello	(BRA)	131	Williams	

DRIVERS

- 76 Michael Schumacher (GER)
- 41 Alain Prost (FRA)
- 39 Kimi Raikkonen (FIN)
- 30 Nigel Mansell (GBR)
- 28 Jim Clark (GBR)
- 25 Mika Hakkinen (FIN)
- 24 Niki Lauda (AUT)
- 23 Juan Manuel Fangio (ARG)
-     Nelson Piquet (BRA)
- 22 Sebastian Vettel (GER)
- 21 Fernando Alonso (SPA)
-     Gerhard Berger (AUT)
- 19 Damon Hill (GBR)
-     Stirling Moss (GBR)
-     Ayrton Senna (BRA)

-     Mark Webber (AUS)
- 18 David Coulthard (GBR)
- 17 Rubens Barrichello (BRA)
- 15 Felipe Massa (BRA)
-     Clay Regazzoni (SWI)
-     Jackie Stewart (GBR)
- 14 Jacky Ickx (BEL)
- 13 Alberto Ascari (ITA)
-     Lewis Hamilton (GBR)
-     Alan Jones (AUS)
-     Riccardo Patrese (ITA)
- 12 Rene Arnoux (FRA)
-     Jack Brabham (AUS)
-     Juan Pablo Montoya (COL)
- 11 John Surtees (GBR)

CONSTRUCTORS

- 228 Ferrari
- 152 McLaren
- 131 Williams
- 71 Lotus
- 54 Lotus* (including Toleman, Benetton, Renault II)
- 41 Red Bull
- 40 Brabham
- 22 Tyrrell
- 18 Renault
- 15 BRM
-     Maserati
- 14 Alfa Romeo
- 13 Cooper
- 12 Matra
-     Mercedes GP (including Brawn GP + BAR + Honda Racing)
-     Prost (including Ligier)

MOST POINTS (THIS FIGURE IS GROSS TALLY, I.E. INCLUDING SCORES THAT WERE LATER DROPPED)

DRIVERS

- 1606 Fernando Alonso (SPA)
- 1566 Michael Schumacher (GER)
- 1451 Sebastian Vettel (GER)
- 1102 Lewis Hamilton (GBR)
- 1072 Jenson Button (GBR)
- 1047.5 Mark Webber (AUS)
- 969 Kimi Raikkonen (FIN)
- 816 Felipe Massa (BRA)
- 798.5 Alain Prost (FRA)
- 658 Rubens Barrichello (BRA)
- 614 Ayrton Senna (BRA)
- 570.5 Nico Rosberg (GER)
- 535 David Coulthard (GBR)
- 485.5 Nelson Piquet (BRA)
- 482 Nigel Mansell (GBR)
- 420.5 Niki Lauda (AUT)
- 420 Mika Hakkinen (FIN)
- 385 Gerhard Berger (AUT)

- 360 Damon Hill (GBR)
-     Jackie Stewart (GBR)
- 329 Ralf Schumacher (GER)
- 310 Carlos Reutemann (ARG)
- 307 Juan Pablo Montoya (COL)
- 289 Graham Hill (GBR)
- 281 Emerson Fittipaldi (BRA)
-     Riccardo Patrese (ITA)
- 277.5 Juan Manuel Fangio (ARG)
- 275 Giancarlo Fisichella (ITA)
- 274 Jim Clark (GBR)
- 273 Robert Kubica (POL)
- 261 Jack Brabham (AUS)
- 259 Nick Heidfeld (GER)
- 255 Jody Scheckter (RSA)
- 248 Denny Hulme (NZL)
- 246.5 Jarno Trulli (ITA)
- 242 Jean Alesi (FRA)

CONSTRUCTORS

- 5600.5 Ferrari
- 4809.5 McLaren
- 2761 Williams
- 2548.5 Red Bull (including Stewart + Jaguar Racing)
- 2457.5 Lotus* (including Toleman, Benetton, Renault II)
- 1514 Lotus
- 1384 Mercedes GP (including BAR, Honda Racing, Brawn GP)
- 854 Brabham
- 767 Sauber (including BMW Sauber)
- 628 Force India (including Jordan + Midland + Spyker)
- 617 Tyrrell
- 439 BRM
- 424 Prost (including Ligier)
- 333 Cooper
- 312 Renault
- 278.5 Toyota
- 207 Toro Rosso
- 171.5 March
- 167 Arrows
- 155 Matra

Fernando Alonso's fourth place for Ferrari in the 2013 Japanese GP moved him past Michael Schumacher's points record.

Michael Schumacher scored his first F1 win in Belgium, for Benetton in 1992, but didn't claim the first of his seven drivers' titles until 1994.

MOST DRIVERS' TITLES

7	Michael Schumacher	(GER)		Jim Clark	(GBR)	Denis Hulme	(NZL)
5	Juan Manuel Fangio	(ARG)		Emerson Fittipaldi	(BRA)	James Hunt	(GBR)
4	Alain Prost	(FRA)		Mika Hakkinen	(FIN)	Alan Jones	(AUS)
	Sebastian Vettel	(GER)		Graham Hill	(GBR)	Nigel Mansell	(GBR)
3	Jack Brabham	(AUS)	**1**	Mario Andretti	(USA)	Kimi Raikkonen	(FIN)
	Niki Lauda	(AUT)		Jenson Button	(GBR)	Jochen Rindt	(AUT)
	Nelson Piquet	(BRA)		Giuseppe Farina	(ITA)	Keke Rosberg	(FIN)
	Ayrton Senna	(BRA)		Lewis Hamilton	(GBR)	Jody Scheckter	(RSA)
	Jackie Stewart	(GBR)		Mike Hawthorn	(GBR)	John Surtees	(GBR)
2	Fernando Alonso	(SPA)		Damon Hill	(GBR)	Jacques Villeneuve	(CDN)
	Alberto Ascari	(ITA)		Phil Hill	(USA)		

MOST CONSTRUCTORS' TITLES

16	Ferrari	**2**	Brabham		BRM
9	Williams		Cooper		Matra
8	McLaren		Renault		Tyrrell
7	Lotus	**1**	Benetton		Vanwall
4	Red Bull		Brawn		

NB To avoid confusion in the number of race starts that teams have contested, the Lotus figures listed are for the team that ran from 1958 to 1994, whereas those listed as Lotus* are for the team based at Enstone that started as Toleman in 1981, became Benetton in 1986 then Renault in 2002 and Lotus in 2012. The Renault listings are for the team that ran from 1977 to 1985, the stats for Red Bull Racing include those of the Stewart Grand Prix and Jaguar Racing teams from which it evolved, those for Mercedes GP for the team that started as BAR in 1999, then ran as Honda GP from 2006 and as Brawn GP in 2009. Force India's stats include those of Jordan, Midland and Spyker, while Scuderia Toro Rosso's include those of its forerunner Minardi.

2014 FILL-IN CHART

DRIVER	TEAM	Round 1 – 16 March AUSTRALIAN GP	Round 2 – 30 March MALAYSIAN GP	Round 3 – 6 April BAHRAIN GP	Round 4 – 20 April CHINESE GP	Round 5 – 11 May SPANISH GP	Round 6 – 25 May MONACO GP	Round 7 – 8 June CANADIAN GP	Round 8 – 22 June AUSTRIAN GP
1 SEBASTIAN VETTEL	Red Bull								
2 DANIEL RICCIARDO	Red Bull								
3 FERNANDO ALONSO	Ferrari								
4 KIMI RAIKKONEN	Ferrari								
5 NICO ROSBERG	Mercedes								
6 LEWIS HAMILTON	Mercedes								
7 ROMAIN GROSJEAN	Lotus								
8 PASTOR MALDONADO	Lotus								
9 JENSON BUTTON	McLaren								
10 KEVIN MAGNUSSEN	McLaren								
11 NICO HULKENBERG	Force India								
12 SERGIO PEREZ	Force India								
14 ADRIAN SUTIL	Sauber								
15 ESTEBAN GUTIERREZ	Sauber								
16 JEAN-ERIC VERGNE	Toro Rosso								
17 DANIIL KVYAT	Toro Rosso								
18 FELIPE MASSA	Williams								
19 VALTTERI BOTTAS	Williams								
20 JULES BIANCHI	Marussia								
21 MAX CHILTON*	Marussia								
22 HEIKKI KOVALAINEN*	Caterham								
23 GIEDO VAN DER GARDE*	Caterham								

SCORING SYSTEM: 25, 18, 15, 12, 10, 8, 6, 4, 2, 1 POINTS
FOR THE FIRST 10 FINISHERS IN EACH GRAND PRIX, WITH
DOUBLE POINTS ALLOCATED FOR THE FINAL ROUND.

* UNCONFIRMED AT TIME OF GOING TO PRESS

Round 9 – 6 July BRITISH GP	Round 10 – 20 July GERMAN GP	Round 11 – 27 July HUNGARIAN GP	Round 12 – 24 Aug BELGIAN GP	Round 13 – 7 Sep ITALIAN GP	Round 14 – 21 Sep SINGAPORE GP	Round 15 – 5 Oct JAPANESE GP	Round 16 – 12 Oct RUSSIAN GP	Round 17 – 2 Nov UNITED STATES GP	Round 18 – 9 Nov BRAZILIAN GP	Round 19 – 23 Nov ABU DHABI GP	POINTS TOTAL

To the delight of the home crowd, Fernando Alonso takes the chequered flag to win the 2013 Spanish GP for Ferrari.

The publishers would like to thank the following sources for
their kind permission to reproduce the pictures in this book.

Getty Images: /Clive Mason: 117; /Ker Robertson: 93; /Clive Rose: 111

LAT Photographic: 63R, 63B, 65TR, 120, 121, 122, 123, 125; /Sam Bloxham: 45; /Charles Coates:
20, 23, 26, 27, 31, 43, 51, 54, 55, 58, 59, 60, 61, 94-95, 97, 99, 115, 128; /Glenn Dunbar: 12, 16, 32-33,
48, 49, 52, 66-67, 76-77, 110, 113; /Steve Etherington: 8-9, 14, 15, 17, 101, 104, 106, 112; /Andrew
Ferraro: 25, 42, 53; /Andy Hone: 10, 11, 24, 30, 34, 36, 38, 44, 46-47, 50, 65B, 98, 100, 114, 116, 124; /
Jed Leicester: 18-19, 105; /Tony Smythe: 65TL; /Alastair Staley: 3, 5, 28, 96, 109; /Steven Tee: 6-7,
13, 21, 22, 29, 37, 40, 41, 56-57, 68-69, 84-85, 102-103, 107, 108

Press Association Images: /James Moy Photography: 35

© **Renault:** 63TL

© **Sauber Motorsport:** 39

Every effort has been made to acknowledge correctly and contact the source and/or
copyright holder of each picture and Carlton Books Limited apologises for any unintentional
errors or omissions that will be corrected in future editions of this book.